U.S.A. 2012: After the Middle-Class Revolution

U.S.A. 2012

After the Middle-Class Revolution

Kenneth M. Dolbeare

Janette Kay Hubbell

Chatham House Publishers, Inc.
Chatham, New Jersey

U.S.A. 2012: After the Middle-Class Revolution

Chatham House Publishers, Inc.
Post Office Box One
Chatham, New Jersey 07928

Copyright © 1996 by Chatham House Publishers, Inc.

Publisher: Edward Artinian
Jacket and cover design: Lawrence Ratzkin
Production supervisor: Katharine Miller
Composition: Bang, Motley, Olufsen
Printing and binding: R.R. Donnelley & Sons Company

Library of Congress Cataloging-in-Publication Data

Dolbeare, Kenneth M.
    U.S.A. 2012: after the middle-class revolution /
Kenneth M. Dolbeare, Janette Kay Hubbell.
        p.   cm.
    Includes bibliographical references and index.
    ISBN 1-56643-036-4. — ISBN 1-56643-035-6 (pbk.)
    1. Economic forecasting—United States.   2. United
States—Economic policy—1993–   3. Middle class—United
States.   I. Hubbell, Janette Kay, 1948–   .   II. Title.
HC106.82.D65   1996
330. 973′001′12—dc20   95-50207
                                                           CIP

Manufactured in the United States of America
10   9   8   7   6   5   4   3   2   1

To our children and (new) grandchild:
Beth, Jake, Joey, Lindsay, Matt, Patty, and Tim

Contents

Part I. Problems and Prospects

Figures and Tables

Preface

O ur premise in this book is that the United States has been for the past two decades in the midst of an economic-social-cultural transformation in which the middle class has paid a heavy economic price in the way of lost jobs, insecurity, and an increasingly threatening future. Our intended audience is the 70 million American families who earn between $25,000 and $100,000 a year, and particularly their sons and daughters, who must live in that future. We envision a drastic middle-class Jeffersonian revolution—a fundamental shift toward economic nationalism and the basic political reconstruction that will enable it. We believe this is the only alternative to thirty more years of economic hardship and decline for millions of Americans and the only solution to our current problems that will preserve and enhance the democratic features of our society. Other, far less attractive alternatives are more likely prospects, but they are not inevitable. Despite the low odds, we believe Americans still have a chance to turn things around.

A significant part of the problem of change is that ordinary middle-class people do not think of themselves as purposeful historical actors, as people who consciously make the history that later generations will read about and understand as "history." This may be a result of the detached and self-justifying way that history is written by the winners and their supporters. Everything sounds like it was predestined or inevitable and was accomplished by heroic leaders, whereas in reality it was a set of choices and bitter conflicts between real people.

This is why we employ the literary device of a college student in search of his own understanding of the turn-of-the-century years from the perspective of 2012. Every chapter begins with a fictional vignette of David's inquiry into the way that the world of 2012 was achieved by members of his parents' generation. These ordinary adults, acting with faith in their friends and spiritual communities in the midst of growing chaos and uncertainty, effectively saved their country from a spiral of decline and disintegration. We want to recapture the hopes and fears, daring determination, and sacrifice of leaders and citizens alike during those exciting years. Fiction is the only way, and we ask the reader's indulgence and participation.

The authors are an eastern iconoclast who teaches politics at a small college and a southwestern populist who left elementary school teaching to launch a successful small business. We live now in the Pacific Northwest, but our hopes and fears are the same as those of people like us anywhere. Our children, both the college graduates among them and those still struggling through, face a future far more uncertain and challenging than anything in our experience. We write with them in mind.

Our program fits no category of current American political thinking known to us. We use the concept of nationalism benignly to mean (1) American society as a whole, as an organic community distinct from other social units in the world, that is (2) made up of *people,* particularly the great bulk of Americans in the middle of the social pyramid, rather than corporations and special interests. Our nationalism is democratic, not authoritarian. It has little in common with Teddy Roosevelt's usage of the term and only a remote connection with Edward Bellamy's once-famous *Looking Backward.*

Our guess is that something like this program is already growing in the minds of millions of Americans and that we will prove to be only one of many voices in its behalf. When their time comes, good ideas appear simultaneously from many sources. Indeed, when we submitted the first draft of this manuscript to our publisher, he called our attention to the Tofflers' *Creating a New Civilization: The Politics of the Third Wave,* which at the time we had not read. There are several similarities, particularly regarding Jeffersonian democracy, but we think we go beyond the Tofflers (as well as all the other contemporary political prescriptions) in many respects.

We readily recognize that no program of economic nationalism can be enacted by the U.S. government today, for at least two reasons. One is that the multinational corporations and banks have the institutions of the national government completely locked up by their web of lobbying, campaign funding, and regular threats of capital flight or loss of "business confidence."

The other reason is that most people have lost any hope or expectation that their government can do *anything* well. This conclusion is in some respects justified, in part because of the way that the present corporate owners have used the government for their own private advantage. But it is also the result of relentless attacks on government sponsored by those so wealthy that they do not want or need it—and implemented by their eager political servants. Government has been made the scapegoat for the problems of the country.

Much new self-reliance by individual Americans is required, to be sure, but an effective government must also be available as an instrument of the people. Major political reforms will be necessary for the national government to be placed under the direct democratic control of the American people. That is the only way to restore confidence that it will do what the people want. The political system is hopelessly unresponsive today, and without basic reconstruction will only get worse. The only way to enact an economic nationalist program is to make major issues subject to popular decision after due debate and reflection, firmly restrict campaign funding, open elections to multiple political parties and proportional voting, and generally make a direct and issue-based democracy possible for the first time.

The centerpiece of our program for political reconstruction is a procedure for regular and binding popular decision making on all major national issues. We envision quarterly voting weekends, with from two to four major issues at stake on each occasion. Carefully framed text and explanations of the proposal will be made available by a nonpartisan source at least sixty days prior to the vote in order to assure adequate time for ample public debate and thoughtful consideration before the decisions are made. Once made, Congress and president will be required to implement such decisions in good faith. We offer a procedure for identifying "major issues," alternatively by either house of Congress or by a specified number of voters. All of the procedures proposed are improvements on experience with initiatives and referenda in the states, and we advocate trial usage of this popular decision-making procedure in several states prior to instituting it on the national level. But it should be clear that neither the amateurishness nor the time-consuming signature gathering of the current initiative process will be involved in this new procedure: instead, every major issue will be *routinely* presented to the voters for their informed and binding judgment. We argue that the notion of representation is an eighteenth-century concept in need of adaptation in light of multiple forms of new electronic communications technology and the profound crisis of legitimacy of the current American political system.

These may at first seem to be outrageous proposals. Given the goal of restoring decent living conditions and prospects for the majority of Americans and avoiding Third World status for the country, however, these are the *only* alternatives adequate to the problems we face. To do less is to acquiesce in continued decline. Even if such a program is ultimately overwhelmed by global change, it will have eased the transition for many millions of people in the interim.

Addressing these problems requires a new way of thinking about our problems and prospects. The year 2012 is not so far away: from the present to 2012 is less than one generation and about the same time that elapsed between the "business as usual" election of 1928 and the dramatic changes of the New

Deal and World War II era that were completed by 1944. Comparing the governmental role of 1928 with that of 1944 is truly a night-and-day experience; even more change is likely between the present and 2012.

In order to promote readability we have deliberately avoided citations to sources and authorities in the text. In the bibliographic essay, however, the reader can find both citations and an annotated bibliography of the best works in this field.

We want to record our thanks to some readers of early versions of this book whose suspension of disbelief and outright encouragement were crucial to completion: Dan, Kim, Mike, and June made vital contributions.

' ...To equality... '

ONE

Thomas Jefferson Revisited: The Fourth of July, 2000

David eased his rented three-wheeler into an opening in the automatic lane of the freeway, tuned in the autopilot frequency, and locked it in. He yawned and stretched with a pleasant combination of relaxation and anticipation. Three of the four hours of his trip would be on autopilot at a steady 70 miles per hour, giving him time to prepare carefully for what was starting to become for him the most interesting assignment of his college experience.

He flicked on the monitor, shoved the videocassette of the lecture describing the assignment into the car's VCR, and opened his notebook. Although he had actually cut the lecture to recover from an all-night party, the student note-taking service sold high-quality tapes that were actually better than the real thing. Probably they edited out some of the instructor's repetitiveness and distracting mannerisms.

In this Thanksgiving vacation of his sophomore year, as part of a course in political journalism, David had to conduct some in-depth interviews with his parents. The subject assigned was the experience of the previous generation amid the dramatic changes occurring in the United States in the sixteen years between 1996 and the present, and how they felt about it today.

The thirty students in the class were all doing the same task this weekend, and in the remaining weeks of the course they would try to combine their results into a people's history of that great upheaval.

In particular, David and the other students were directed to inquire about three issues: (1) What date or event did people recognize today as the moment when a revolutionary process actually started? (2) When did people *realize* that they were involved in a revolution (in the sense of the scope of change involved), and what really gave them the anger, courage, hope, fear, or whatever motivated them to take part? What did they *do,* and why? (3) How did people *feel* at various stages of the process, up to the present postelection moment in 2012? Were they ever really discouraged or afraid, or both, that one of the other possible alternatives would emerge from all the chaos and uncertainty? What was the single most important step they took? And why was it so important?

The instructor posed as a possible thesis that the revolution should be dated from the time of the approval of the New Declaration of Independence on the Fourth of July, 2000, by the several independent political parties and citizen groups that had been working on it. She distributed copies of the famous document so that students would all have it available for use in their interviews. David scrolled the text on the videotape, recalling some passages and seeing others with new curiosity. He was increasingly skeptical that anything like this could have been produced except by a pretty well organized movement that had been under way for at least a couple of years. When did a "revolution" actually begin, and where—in people's heads, in the streets, or at great moments like a Fourth of July? That was an interesting question!

Actually, David had been alive for all of this time—he was born in 1993—but of course he had not been aware of what was happening in economics or politics or social life generally until the past few years. But both his parents had come to their political awareness shortly before graduation from college in the Reagan years of the 1980s. They were still actively involved, even though both had recently passed their fiftieth birthdays. His dad was in his fourth "new career," now as a computer consultant helping small businesses stay up to date; his mom was a lawyer specializing in keeping people out of court. But both were defined by their roles in various community networks and not by their occupations.

David knew they would be very good informants; besides, in contrast to many of his friends, he really liked his parents and looked forward to reconstructing their life experiences with them. He also wanted very much to understand how people who had some knowledge of the 1990s would understand the tumultuous years of the early twenty-first century.

T̲ens of millions of Americans are suffering from unprecedented economic pressures, and they are frustrated and angry. They have every right to be. They have done the work, fought the wars, and played by the rules, only to be confronted by corruption, greed, crime, and a very uncertain future for their children. We briefly show how this happened and then how middle Americans themselves have contributed to it. Finally, we describe how they can transform themselves from victims into revolutionaries and explain the book that follows.

The Betrayal of the Middle Class

Middle-class values are by definition those of the American mainstream: *individualism,* in the sense of self-reliance, personal dignity and respect, and taking responsibility for oneself and one's family; *opportunity,* meaning the chance to rise above one's origins through hard work, thrift, good character, and playing by the rules; *property,* as a primary goal, the acquisition of which assures independence, a stake in the society, and the prospect of a better life for one's children; *freedom*, from all but really necessary restraints, as the right to choose one's own directions in life; and *equality*, in the sense of genuine availability of opportunities to all without special preferences, and equal and effective weight in politics.

These are the values and beliefs that built the mythical American Dream that attracted millions of aspiring immigrants from all over the world. They also built the United States into the most powerful and most resource-consuming nation in the history of the planet. The interests of the great bulk of the American middle class, and those of the giant corporations and banks rising with them at the end of World War II, seemed to converge.

The Erosion Begins

Then the world changed. Technology permitted and corporations built a new version of a global capitalist economy. Capital relocated rapidly to low-wage regions of the world, leaving employees jobless and their communities destitute. Quick transportation of goods and services to distant markets became possible, and suddenly the U.S. market was flooded with inexpensive foreign-made goods of reasonable quality. More jobs were lost, and American workers were blamed for being too demanding and "uncompetitive."

The American standard of living began to erode, despite two-income family efforts, and the middle class began to shrink—a few moving up, but many moving down into near-poverty. The American Dream receded from reality in the course of three short decades. The newly transnational corporations and banks in essence turned on the American middle class and broke its grip on the economic ladder. Profits shot up as wages dropped; stock prices increased with every layoff.

Middle-Class Images

While real wages held constant or fell for nearly all Americans, the very rich were reaping huge gains. One-half of one percent of

U.S. households, about 500,000 families, owned about 40 per-cent of all assets in the country, making the United States the world leader in inequality of income. Moreover, as the net worth of the country grew from 1983 to 1989, more than half the growth was taken by this same .5 percent of families—on aver-age, about $3.9 million increase per family in a six-year period. Lurid tales of vast commissions achieved by stockbrokers and in-vestment houses filled the news media. Particularly galling was the tens of millions of dollars paid to junk-bond salesmen who engineered takeovers that resulted in job cuts and corporate downsizing.

At the bottom of the social pyramid were rising welfare costs and crime rates. Welfare populations were seen as permanent, willfully indigent burdens on an increasingly hard-pressed body of taxpayers. Perceptions held that welfare recipients were able-bodied but lazy, predominantly minorities, and in many in-stances promiscuous women producing babies with a different father every year. Although these images were wrong, political leaders constantly repeated them.

At the same time, drug usage and crime rates steadily in-creased. In 1963 the FBI reported 2,180 crimes for every 100,000 people; thirty years later, the rate was 5,483—an in-crease of more than 150 percent. Juvenile arrests for violent crime rose 68 percent between 1984 and 1993. Almost a million criminals were in state and federal prisons in 1995, more than double the number in 1985, but it seemed to have little effect. Americans ranked crime as the greatest national problem in 1995, and 89 percent said the crime problem was getting worse.

Bipartisan Public Policy Attacks
the Middle Class

One of the truly great fraud-and-hypocrisy posturings of all time was the claim of either the Democratic or the Republican Party to serve as the representative of the American middle class. The rhetoric of middle-class concern resounded across the land, dur-ing electoral campaigns and at every other opportunity. The real-ity was—as the middle class suspected—that both parties used that rhetoric to cover their systematic looting of the middle class on behalf of the particular special interests that they really represented. We offer two tax policy illustrations from the thousands begging to be made visible, both of them (of course) completely bipartisan in origin and implementation.

1. *Thirty years of tax policy.* In the 1950s, with a relatively progressive tax system, corporations and the wealthy paid a substantial share of federal taxes. Borrowing, which transfers money from average taxpayers to the wealthy who have the money to buy Treasury bonds, was at a minimum. Payroll taxes, regressive taxes that hit the lower incomes proportionally harder than the higher incomes, were a small proportion of federal revenues. Moreover, state taxing systems, most of which were linked to and thus mirrored the federal income tax, were therefore relatively progressive, although they also relied on (regressive) sales and property taxes.

After the 1950s, however, a succession of Democratic and Republican presidents, and mostly Democratic Congresses, totally reshaped the nation's taxing system to shift the burden from the upper levels to the middle class. Figure 1.1 (p. 8) documents this shift in stark fashion. In the 1950s, there were a significant corporate income tax, significant estate taxes on the transfer of great wealth from one generation to the next, and relatively low payroll taxes and borrowing. By the end of the 1980s, however, this trend had been totally reversed. Corporate income taxes had been cut by 75 percent, and estate taxes by 50 percent. Payroll taxes had nearly tripled, and borrowing had leaped by more than 900 percent.

This same story can be told with another set of contrasts. In the 1950s, the median-income family's effective federal tax rate (income tax plus payroll tax) was less than 10 percent, while the effective rate on the top 1 percent was more than 85 percent. In what Kevin Phillips calls "The Great Tax-Rate Turnaround," these rates were roughly equalized by the end of the 1980s. Phillips says,

[A]n extraordinary convergence was taking place: the effective combined rate of federal taxes (income, excise, and payroll) on median or average families had climbed to the 25–28 percent range, depending on the calculation, while the rate on households with $500,000 incomes had declined to roughly 28 percent. There, in a sentence, was the fiscal revolution ... the tax changes ... reduced the bite on the rich and increased it on the average family. In less than a generation, the average American went from being a political icon to being a fiscal milch cow.

This shift was arguably one of the most dramatic peaceful transfers of wealth in all of human history. It seems unlikely that the middle class volunteered to be skewered for the benefit of the rich in this manner. Could this steady thirty-year policy shift have been unintentional, the inadvertent act of officeholders whose dedicated attention was focused on other ways of serving their constituents? Or was it owed in major part to the deliberate and purposeful actions of politicians of the Democratic and Republican parties—and, of course, to the financial elite who control both parties?

2. *Thirty years of tax "reform."* Congress regularly enacts tax "reforms" presented with great fanfare as moves toward "fairness" and "simplification." The Pulitzer prize-winning authors Donald Barlett and James Steele show in bitter detail in their *America: Who Really Pays the Taxes?* that tax changes justified with the label of "reforms" have *always and systematically* been new versions of shifting the tax burden from the wealthy to the middle class.

Among other points, they show that the federal government uses a share of Social Security tax revenues—paid only on the first $62,700 of annual income—to cover daily operating costs of the government (rather than build up the trust fund intended for contributors' retirement). One result is that middle-income families pay for this share of the government's operating costs at a ratio up to 90 times that of high-paid corporate execu-

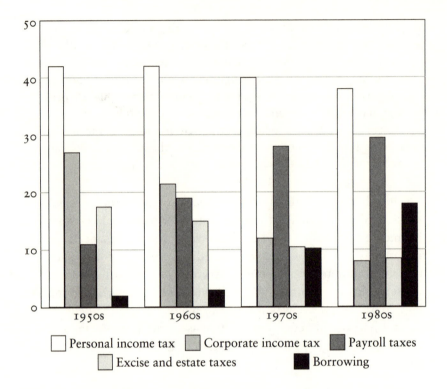

FIGURE 1.1
SOURCE OF FUNDS FOR FEDERAL SPENDING
(AVERAGE ANNUAL SHARES BY DECADES)

SOURCE: Robert J. Shapiro, "Paying for Progress," Progressive Policy Institute, February 1991. Derived from *Budget of the United States Government, 1991, Historical Tables, 1.1, 2.2.*

tives. Barlett and Steele sum up tax "reform" efforts in this manner:

> [A]nalysis of a half century of tax and economic data shows that to pull off this sleight of hand, a succession of Congresses and Presidents has issued a blizzard of sometimes obscure, sometimes misleading, and, increasingly, false statements on government finances.... So it is that while politicians and economists each year argue over the proper mix of spending cuts and tax increases to curb the federal deficit, they have concealed a much larger issue: For more than two decades, a collection of Congresses and Presidents of both parties have transferred the overall tax burden in the United States from the people at the top of the economic ladder to those in the middle and, in many cases, at the bottom. They have done this in two ways:
> First, by dramatically increasing Social Security tax rates and then using the money for ordinary government programs—not social security—while simultaneously cutting the tax bills of the nation's most affluent citizens by billions of dollars.
> Second, by shifting the cost of billions of dollars in programs once underwritten by the federal government to state and local governments, whose tax systems impose a much heavier burden on people in the middle and at the bottom.

When fifty years of changes in public policy consistently tend in the same direction, it is hard to see the results as anything other than the purposeful intention of a permanent set of governing elites.

Thirty Years of Partisan Politics

The story of the past thirty years of American party politics, as far as the middle class is concerned, is a story of explicit promises violated and implicit commitments repudiated, first by the Democrats and then by the Republicans. It is not a pretty picture.

For the three decades prior to 1965, the New Deal and successor regimes taxed the rich and made government programs available to middle- and working-class people on a universal and social insurance basis. Starting, however, with Lyndon Johnson's Great Society, government programs began selectively to target the poor and black—and to lose the vital support of the white middle. What began as universalistic help for all soon seemed like special advantages for a relative few.

The war in Vietnam began to absorb the nation's capital, both financial and human, and to ignite inflation. By 1968, the combination of the war and a Wallace-led reaction against perceived preference for the poor and black began to draw key components away from the Democratic Party. Catholics, skilled workers generally and union members particularly, the white South—a broad swath of the middle class—began an exodus that was dramatically confirmed in the landslide election of 1972. The Democratic Party became a shell of its former self, made up principally of internationalist financial elites, liberal professionals, politicians, and the poor and black, with a scattering of loyalists from the old constituencies.

Less often recognized with respect to this period (1964–72) was the near-collapse of the people's confidence in their government. Levels of confidence that the government could be trusted to do what is right, that it worked for the people and not for a few big interests, that politicians cared about "what people like me think," in Congress and in the executive branch all fell by roughly half between 1964 and 1972. Voting turnout dropped more than 5 percent between 1968 and 1972, though some of this was attributable to low turnout by the newly enfranchised 18–21 year olds.

The war and repeated lying on the part of the presidents and key officials of both parties were only partial causes of the profound alienation that took hold in this period. The middle class was also reacting against riots, preferences for the poor and black, and what appeared to be a broken contract for growth, stability, and opportunity for all.

Republicans had one opportunity to restore faith in government and build a permanent base of support after 1972, but they squandered it in the Watergate scandal. With Nixon's resignation in the face of impeachment, the Democrats and their southern candidate had a brief revival in 1974–76. Lacking ideas and leadership, and disabled by inflation, unemployment, and oil and hostage crises, the Democrats handed a new opportunity to the Republicans under Reagan.

The Reagan appeal was broad, and the rhetoric of restoration of American prestige and prosperity was very powerful when delivered by a man of such innocence and sincerity. His antitax and proreligious positions added to the scope of his appeal. The landslide election of 1984 seemed to show that he was on the verge of cementing the key Democratic constituencies to the Republican Party. But the idea that celebrating business and the rich could bring prosperity to the middle and working classes began to falter as early as 1988, and Bush succeeded to the presidency by a combination of momentum and a racist campaign aided by the gift of Dukakis's ineptitude.

With the recession of the early 1990s and growing evidence of greed and profiteering at the top, Republican support from the middle and working classes dropped sharply. Another round of frustration, cynicism, and alienation ensued, some of it vented in the three-way campaign of 1992. The standard confidence measures all dropped sharply again, to the levels noted earlier in this chapter. Voter turnout increased 5 percent over the sixty-four-year low set in 1988, but it was dissatisfaction and anger with the parties and the government that motivated voters. An even greater frustration lay behind the 1994 results, which gave the Republicans still another opportunity to try to hold the support of middle- and working-class voters while transferring their remaining wealth to the already rich.

The story of the past thirty years of partisan politics is thus one of repeated failure on the part of both parties to address the real economic problems of the country. Neither has responded to the felt needs of the middle class; instead, both have continued the thirty-year pattern of tax "reform," erosion of the middle-class standard of living, and transfer of the tax burden from the rich to the middle and lower levels. There are ample divisive cultural appeals, particularly racial and religious ones, from voices on the right. But nobody speaks sincerely for the economic needs of the middle class. The American political system has not delivered and seems incapable of doing so. The game is rigged: why should people play?

Acquiescence and Victimization

It may seem incredible that two generations of American political leaders would thus target the solid, dependable middle of their society. But it is just as incredible that middle Americans would *let* them do it, and even play the role of helpless or diverted victims while it was going on. They did, however, and it is time to learn some lessons from the ways that it happened.

Individualism Displaces Community and Social Purpose

The strength of American individualism lies in self-reliance and personal responsibility and in a connection between the individual and the larger society of which he or she is a part. Even in the days of the celebrated "rugged individual," that individual was tied closely to others in cooperative relationships that acknowledged shared goals.

In the past thirty years, however, individualism has been exaggerated and corrupted. Self-interest to the point of selfishness and self-indulgence, isolation and denial of community responsibilities, and materialism and consumerism have come to define what it means to be an individual. This new version explains widespread withdrawal from civic and public life, the abandonment of unions, and a general denial of responsibility to or for others. Extended only slightly, individualism is used to justify separatism, fragmentation by ethnic, racial, or religious groupings, and cultural distinctiveness over shared characteristics of the whole society.

But nobody seems to notice or care that this central commitment of American culture has been so drastically reshaped. Social purpose, in the sense of goals requiring collective action, seems to be a historical relic dating back to World War II. To be sure, there has been powerful and at times overwhelming inducement in the form of advertising and television presentations to accept this corrupted version of individualism. But we have in some ways welcomed absorption into consumer society and its relentless emphasis on material acquisitions and new forms of entertainment. Part of today's middle American frustration and anger is certainly owed to having (perhaps innocently) bought into this image of individualism—and with it the inability to grasp any other.

A curious corollary to the new individualism is a willingness to let government do many things that individuals used to do either for themselves or for one another. More and more responsibility has been eagerly passed to the government, and individual rights to a wide variety of benefits are now viewed as unchangeable. Almost nobody is willing to give up these special rights and claims once they have been established in law. Instead, special-interest lobbying to expand group claims on the society through the government has become a hallmark of our politics.

The Iron Grip of Orthodox Ideology

Americans may be the most heavily ideologized society in the world, with so many beliefs so widely shared and taken for granted as truths that they are not even recognized as an ideology unique to the United States. Our ideology tells us, for example, that the American Constitution is a work of unparalleled genius that erected self-regulating economic and political systems with eternal and unfailing ability to assure prosperity and democracy. We do not acknowledge that 210 years have changed the context or consequences of these systems or draw lessons from the fact that every other social institution has been obliged to make radical adaptations to serve evolving needs.

Instead, we assume that the free market is always the best way to employ resources and distribute burdens and benefits and that it always works fairly and efficiently. Similarly, if something is wrong, it must be solely because some public officials have failed to do their prescribed duties. There can be no flaw in the underlying system, so the problem must lie with public officials who make up today's government.

We assume that the Constitution erected a democracy and that therefore whatever we have fits the definition of "democracy"—or is at least unchangeable. We wear blinders to avoid seeing the dominance of wealthy elites and corporations or the corruption of our politics by big-money campaign contributors and television costs. We refuse to take seriously critiques of our basic systems, and we marginalize those who assert them. In short, we are not responsible citizens. Instead, we are *false patriots*—people who indulge in comforting illusions about the eternal validity of a glorious past in order to avoid the hard necessity of disciplining ourselves and adapting our institutions to assure an equally glorious future for our successors.

Multiple Forms of Avoidance

The grip of ideology may even be secretly welcomed because it tells us what must be true, establishes the bounds of orthodoxy, and offers support for not recognizing or not acting on problems that might otherwise be compelling. Because we know our ideology is correct, we can engage in denial for long periods of time or blame individual officeholders for broad social failures for which we share responsibility. Or we can willingly accept as valid the deliberate half-truths of public officials and candidates because they are consistent with our underlying beliefs. We want so much to believe in our system that we accept systematic lying in preference to truth: this is the lesson of Vietnam and any number of illegal or corrupt acts and their cover-ups.

But the greatest avoidance of all is our deliberate insulation from politics and the governance that occurs in our name. Lack of attention, knowledge, and involvement permits and encourages the behavior of leaders and officeholders that, at some point, we finally awake to and deplore. It is certainly true that the major political parties serve as an effective cover for management of the economy and society by wealthy elites and that withdrawal from voting is in a sense rational. But it would make much more sense to organize and take back the government from its present owners.

Yet the idea of organizing with others in political parties with clear goals and purposes more often than not deflects us still further. Our ideology tells us that "factions" are bad and majorities are dangerous, and it warns against the "tyranny of the majority." Our individualism denies that worthy goals are to be realized from collective action, and cost-benefit analysis says that we could use the time more profitably on our own. If quick victories from social efforts are not achieved, moreover, we are soon off to other gratifications.

Scapegoating, Particularly Government

Simple solutions are always attractive, particularly when they are grounded in deep-running cultural currents. Americans have always been suspicious of governments, hostile to other races, and ready to suspect unfamiliar religions (or worse, the lack of any religious ties). Symbols and stereotypes representing such tensions run through our language and are readily available for creative use to deflect attention from fundamental economic, social, or political issues.

Recently, political leaders have strongly encouraged Americans to believe that the problems they feel are caused by governments, particularly the federal government. Some problems certainly have been, as bureaucrats sought to micromanage and social-engineer any number of "good things." But the issue really is, *who controls the government?* At present, the U.S. government is an often willing captive of the major corporations and banks and the nation's wealthiest people. It is their government that is doing the kinds of things described above, not ours.

The best response is to take back control of the government and then to make it work the people's will. There is no way that middle Americans can realize goals involving economic prosperity and a secure future *without* an effective government able to act in their name. To disable or destroy the only source of achieving social goals is the ultimate act of self-destruction—and one very much desired by those who are so wealthy that they do not need an effective government (and, of course, their vocal political servants).

From Victims to Revolutionaries

We need to learn some lessons before it is too late—before our country declines further or disintegrates into warring factions. There are remedies for our problems, and they are achievable. They require many of us to change the way we think and act, to find one another as members of a national community with shared purposes, and to regain our faith in the future that our children deserve.

Americans have great economic, social, and political strengths and, more important, deep moral and cultural resources. The twenty-first century could be an American century that would eclipse our past in moral and material achievement. With a combination of a collective spiritual awakening and personal assumption of responsibility, Americans could learn to act as an organic community in our long-term common interest. For more than 200 years, Alexander Hamilton's government has grown and prospered by doing things for us. It is past time to take up Thomas Jefferson's challenge to trust ourselves and, working together, do things for ourselves and our future.

Our purpose in this book is to grasp what is happening while there is still time to act constructively in the long-term public interest—by which we mean the long-term interest of the heart and soul of the American community, the 70 million American families with incomes between $25,000 and $100,000 a year. To focus on this sector of our population is not to exclude others but to recognize the vital middle as the fulcrum of the future. Those below this income level will gain almost as much from such a priority, while those above will be assured of the stability and markets crucial to their continued success.

We envision an achievable and recognizable future, with environmentally sustainable economic growth, secure and well-paid jobs, an effective and genuinely democratic government, and a social context of mutual tolerance and civility. This future *can* be accomplished, despite the presence of many obstacles and destructive alternatives, by a determined effort to recapture control of the national government on the part of a politically alert and determined middle class.

A first step is to celebrate and embrace what is already taking place: the explicit rejection of the existing party system and many of the ideas, ideologies, and practices of the past. Both major political parties today, Republicans and Democrats, are essentially controlled by corporations, banks, and wealthy individuals from the highest echelons of the American economy and society. A somewhat distinctive mix of such sources actually provides the funding and guidance for each party, but there are few real differences between them. The parties *both* do what business and the wealthy want.

The voters are beginning to understand that and to see the major political parties as being the problem. The elections of 1992 and 1994 make their rejection very clear. But a new majority politics and a new economic program are yet to be found.

A second step is to recognize that our heritage includes many basic values that have served us well and to design both economic programs and political changes to implement them better in today's new context. Vision and program are crucial. Without a vision for the future and a substantive prescription for political and economic changes, both of which carry forward a renewed version of some basic American values, constructive change is impossible.

Middle Americans deserve a program for an essentially Jeffersonian middle-class revolution. In a famous passage, Jefferson once said,

> Some men look at constitutions with sanctimonious reverence, and deem them like the arc of the covenant, too sacred to be touched. They ascribe to the men of the preceding age a wisdom more than human, and suppose what they did to be beyond amendment.... [A]s new discoveries are made, new truths disclosed, and manners and opinions change with the change of circumstances, institutions must change also, and keep pace with the times.... Each generation has then a right to choose for itself the form of government it believes most promotive of its own happiness.... This corporeal globe, and everything upon it, belong to its present corporeal inhabitants, during their generation. They alone have a right to direct what is the concern of

themselves, alone, and to declare the law of that direction; and this declaration can only be made by their majority.... Only lay down true principles, and adhere to them inflexibly. Do not be frightened into their surrender by the alarms of the timid, or the croakings of wealth against the ascendancy of the people.

This consolidated passage is the basis of all that we set forth in the balance of this book. The Constitution belongs to the living, who *must* amend and refine it, for the sake of enabling it to adapt and survive into the future. Only the false patriotism of mindless defenders of the status quo fails to see that the course of true conservatism is carefully considered adaptation and evolution of the essence that makes us what we are today. The Constitution is well into its third century, and the world is changing dramatically: the principles that have served so well need only some fine-tuning, but they need it badly.

This middle-class revolution will be mostly based on the ballot box, although, as in Jefferson's day, there will be additional ways of pressuring the established powers to give up some of their prerogatives. It will replace the current governing elite with a new system implementing Jeffersonian preferences, in which priorities and policies flow directly from the majority of voters. And it will result in a new economic model, one that, while remaining capitalist in character, works more fully for the economic opportunities and benefit of middle- and working-class people.

The contrast with our current system, first put in place by Jefferson's long-standing antagonist, Alexander Hamilton, is inescapable. For Hamilton, the government was to be powerful, centralized, and insulated against popular control. Particularly important was the autonomy of the financial and legal systems, so a financial-commercial elite could better work its will in a highly industrialized system. For more than 200 years, the United States has followed the Hamiltonian path—a path that went terminally astray in the world of the past thirty years.

The time is finally ripe for the Jeffersonian model of a democratic, decentralized, people-focused economic and political system to be implemented in its place. It will be just as American and far more humane. But in the context of what is today, a significant struggle will be required to carry out a problem-solving program involving new national economic policies and a revised constitutional practice. *These are drastic remedies that require that the established structure of power in the country be recognized for what it is and replaced by a government under the direct control of the middle class.*

We stress the last points strongly because they distinguish our analysis and proposals here from every one of the current prescriptions for change in the United States—and probably from any to emerge in the next five years. These works are analyzed in detail in the bibliographic essay, but the basic contrasts must be noted up front.

Our closest comparison is with *Creating a New Civilization: The Politics of the Third Wave,* by the pathbreaking futurists Alvin and Heidi Toffler. This work explicitly links itself to Jefferson and quotes part of the "each generation has a right" passage to justify the prospect of constitutional change. It ignores, however, the urgency of middle-class needs, offers no specific remedies either statutory or constitutional, and assumes that the existing structure of power will graciously change its practices when it sees the light.

More clearly political is the excellent book by Michael Lind, *The Next American Nation: The New Nationalism and the Fourth American Revolution.* Lind sees the class war by the rich against the poor very clearly and notes how the cultural causes mask that reality. He provides a witty and elegant analysis of how "the class that does not exist" rules the country, but he does not address the question of what to do about it except in vague "nationalist" terms.

The best political work of all is that of Kevin Phillips, whose self-styled "populist conservatism" has enabled him to see emerging trends for the past three decades. In his latest work, *Arrogant Capital: Washington, Wall Street, and the Frustration of American Politics,* he offers a very good analysis of the takeover of American government by the new financialism and makes several provocative suggestions for political remedies, such as a national initiative and referendum. His proposals lack grounding in a social movement, however, and do not really address the problem of the current structure of power or how it might be changed.

Several other works take up the current crisis, bemoan the loss of the American Dream and the prospect of Third World status, but offer little in the way of a comprehensive program or a means of changing the structure of power that brought us to this point. These include Ross Perot's *United We Stand: How We Can Take Back Our Country*, Alice Rivlin's *Reviving the American Dream: The Economy, the States, and the Federal Government*, Edward Luttwak's *The Endangered American Dream: How to Stop the United States from Becoming a Third World Country and How to Win the Geo-Economic Struggle for Industrial Supremacy*. All make some interesting analytic points and we draw on them

later. But those authors do not address the real problem: a structure of power that *wants* to keep things the way they are and that has the power to do so. Unfortunately, Newt Gingrich's *To Renew America* and Hedrick Smith's *Rethinking America* fit in this same category.

Although we hope and anticipate that this is only temporary, we can find no other work that embodies our comprehensive program. *A New Declaration of Independence* is a summary of what we envision this revolution to be about—what it is *against,* and what it is *for*—and why and how it will be achieved. In the two chapters of part I, we summarize our present problems and prospects in analytic detail. In the three chapters of part II, we describe a new Jeffersonian system and how it can be realized in the immediate future.

A New Declaration of Independence
Fourth of July, 2000

God has greatly blessed America, but today we the people stand at the brink of desecrating our precious heritage. We ask His support for our rededication to the founding principles of our country and renewal of our fundamental social contract, which will require near-revolutionary change in our institutions and practices. We reaffirm that we are all created equal and are endowed by our Creator with certain inalienable rights, among which are life, liberty, and the pursuit of happiness. We believe in equal rights for all and special privileges for none. We also reaffirm that we are, and of right must be, the sovereign governing force in our society.

Neither of these founding principles is in effect today. Claims for rights without limits dominate our discourse and debase our democracy. Worse, the people are clearly no longer sovereign, and their very capability to be so is derided. Both principles must be revitalized and their balance restored.

We do not lightly seek so fundamentally to change a government long established and once widely respected. But that government has been taken away from us and replaced by a government totally captured by corrupt political parties, career officeholders and bureaucrats, and a multitude of rapacious special interests. After suffering decades of abuses and usurpations, it is our duty and responsibility to restore popular control over that government. Democracy is meaningless unless it *balances* sober popular sovereignty with equal rights exercised with restraint.

We ordain and establish today a new Declaration of Independence such that this nation, under God, shall have a new birth of freedom and responsibility, and government of the people, by the people, and for the people shall bring the United States to new greatness in the twenty-first century.

We declare our independence:

> From the political party system that separates representatives from their constituents and frees them to do whatever their ideologies and campaign contributors dictate

> From domination by the corporations, banks, and wealthy who together control the institutions of our national government and our capital city of Washington, D.C.

> From the television and print media, whose group-think, pandering, and search for scandals have done so much to eliminate principled discussion of issues from our politics

> From the other special interests, whether foreign governments or organized self-interested Americans, who do not give priority to the long-term needs of the children and grandchildren of today's Americans

> From the bureaucracy, of whatever level, which asserts

priority for its own personal convenience and arcane rules
rather than the needs of the citizens of the country

In asserting our new beginning, we must first acknowledge
our debts to our forebears, those whose combination of creativity, hard work, avarice, and sacrifice built the nation we have
proudly inherited. At the same time, we acknowledge that the
process of construction was painful and costly to many racial
and ethnic minorities, particularly Native Americans and African
Americans, and often involved denigration and/or denial of opportunities to women.

These facts granted and regretted, however, we must put
them behind us. We must act together as one people today to recapture our government, restore our economy, and renew our
promise as a community. The only discrimination between
classes or groups tolerable on our joint path to the future is that
which we openly and together decide is necessary to our shared
common interest.

Our new beginning anticipates an American century in which
the equal rights of all will be realized according to individual talent and effort, within the framework provided by our jointly decided social needs and purposes. We dedicate ourselves to environmentally sustainable economic growth, a peaceful and secure
social life, and the challenge of making democracy a reality. This
is the future—and the only future—that our inheritance demands we leave to our children.

To further our new independence, and promote the future of
our shared American community, we offer the following principles for the twenty-first century. We invite all Americans to
join us.

1. We shall organize and act in every way and at every level
   to take back our government: where electoral means are
   appropriate, we shall employ them, but where additional
   means are required, we shall find or make them.

2. We shall establish a politics of issues in which the people shall directly decide all major questions of national public policy after due dialogue and reflection.

3. We shall control the money power with respect to funding political campaigns so that electoral campaigns will be of low cost and brief duration, electoral choices will be unaffected by wealth in any way, and the people's choices will be implemented.

4. We shall break the death grip of today's major parties on our democracy and facilitate the rise of multiple parties and a proportional voting system, such that the true issue and candidate preferences of the people are heard and acted on effectively at every level of government.

5. We shall reallocate the functions of the central government so that many of them are performed in decentralized ways, and/or transferred completely to the states, along with the revenues necessary to accomplish them; we shall reform our courts and law enforcement so that we have far less unproductive law and litigation and far more ability to punish those whose voluntary behavior puts them outside the laws of our community.

6. We shall enact an economic nationalist program on behalf of the middle class, and thereby all Americans, such that jobs and good wages, fairness in taxation and distribution of income, and concern for the long-term future become hallmarks of our revitalized American society.

To these ends, we commit our lives, our fortunes, and our sacred honor. We do so in all humility and to keep faith with our God, our forebears of two centuries ago, and our unborn generations.

Part I

Problems and Prospects

TWO

The United States at the End of the Twentieth Century

David smiled wryly as he tackled the mountain of dishes, pots, pans, and empty containers that were the residue of his father's traditional Thanksgiving Eve chili dinner. The man did make a dynamite chili, great tonight and even better as leftovers for the rest of the weekend, but the mess seemed to get bigger every year. Twice David was interrupted by calls from high school friends trying to get him to join reunions at local taverns. Each time, the television news went mute when the videophone flashed, and he completed his conversations without losing a second from his dish washing. Finally, wiping the counter with a flourish, he looked up to see his mother smiling at him; at least she had the grace to be discreet about checking his work.

Mary Reynolds was a lithe and attractive woman, already fifty but looking more like forty, who was capable of embarrassing both David and his father on the golf course on any given day. But it was an intellectual challenge that she most enjoyed, whether with her family and friends, in her legal work, or in her many community roles. With her usual directness, she said, "David, you've been putting your friends off because you want to start the interviews tonight. I think that's a good idea, because unless you've had a personal transformation, I don't expect to see you before noon tomorrow."

"You're right on all three counts, Counselor," David grinned. "I'll go to the tower and get Dad." The "tower" was the family term for Jeff Reynolds's third-floor technology center, once a bedroom but now a futuristic electronic showplace, crowded with the latest and most powerful computers and communications equipment and wired to the world.

Jeff was a bit older than Mary, but just as physically lively and engaged in his work and the social life of the community. He had started out in the artificial intelligence field, migrated periodically to other cutting-edge areas as they emerged, and never seemed to worry about where or how he would earn his income as long as he was self-employed. He was a kind of philosopher of technology, always asserting the need for people to understand and control its capabilities. Mary liked to watch acquaintances when they first saw the tower and all its equipment: older people's eyes would glaze over and they would retreat mumbling, but younger people would eagerly ask permission and start exploring for themselves, not to be heard from for hours.

Jeff and Mary had each married once right after college and then spent some years as singles ("growing-up time," as they now called the interim) before they met and married in 1990. Their most formative experience, however, occurred when David was in elementary school at the turn of the century. For an intense, exciting, and rewarding several years, they were daily participants in the fundamental reconstruction of their sense of community and of themselves—and, as it turned out, of their country as well. It was a combination of renewal and new beginning, greatly facilitated by the new means of electronic communication.

For these years, and forever after, they were defined not by their backgrounds or occupations or personal characteristics but by what they could and did do on behalf of the future of their community as a whole. It was as if they had been pressure-forged in a crucible of republican citizenship, where individual self-interest and opportunism willingly gave way to joint action to fulfill a shared social purpose—a modern version of the early American concept of "virtue."

David had already explained his assignment to his parents, first on the phone and then at dinner, so he was ready to start as soon as they all got settled comfortably. "I want to know what it was like *before* any of the changes started—in the 1990s, you know; then I want to hear how you first knew that something really *special* was happening."

Jeff and Mary looked at each other, trying to suppress smiles that David might misunderstand. "One at a time, son," Mary said crisply. "They're both huge questions, and your dad and I will want to narrow them first and then answer each separately." She leaned back and took a deep breath as if to start.

"I'll start," Jeff interjected, "and then you'll have something to shoot at." His warm glance at Mary made clear that the intellectual game was on. David was delighted to see that they both were so ready to enjoy themselves and that he was to be included as a participant.

"For starters, the '90s were a launching pad, but far from the beginning. People had been feeling that things were going wrong in every aspect of life for years, ever since the Vietnam war in the 1960s and Watergate in the 1970s. There was a nostalgic 'feel good' surge in the 1980s, but it was soon clear that things were still headed downhill. But there was no clear definition of the core problem or problems—everybody blamed everybody else, particularly governments and taxes, for anything that was different or unsatisfactory in their individual lives.

"Times *were* bad, particularly for middle-aged, middle-class people like your grandparents. Lost jobs, lost pensions, living on one income when two were essential—they went through it all. Your grandpa was laid off and lost his pension, for example. For us, too, times were bad, but we had never known or been promised *good* times, so it was a little easier. Of course, lots of working-class and welfare people had it much tougher than we did."

David was having trouble being patient as his philosopher-father sketched the background he needed before he could get to the question.

His mother's analytic mind did his work for him: "Yes, Jeff, but what was really *distinctive* about the '90s? Why were they *different* from before?"

Jeff plowed on, unruffled. "Well, the financial crash and the depression that began in 1998 were certainly factors. It was the kind of crisis that made absolutely clear that all the old assumptions about how things worked were false and that our world was going to be defined by chaos and uncertainty for years to come. And nobody knew what sort of alternative political and economic system might ultimately take hold—but we all guessed that things were likely to be much worse than they ever had been. Another and maybe related factor was that lots of newly registered voters turned against *both* parties, Democrats and Republicans, and demanded the kind of direct democracy we have now, where people vote directly on all major national issues."

Mary intervened in her precise manner: "You're forgetting the single most important catalyst of the decade, the Republican 'Contract with America' in 1994." Turning to David, she added parenthetically, "You know, that wonderfully self-contradictory document that nobody ever heard of until after the voters dumped the Democrats in 1994. The one that the Republicans made such a fuss about and then weren't even embarrassed by, although it was such a windfall for the wealthy."

"Why was that so important?" David asked with real interest. "I've never heard of it." Jeff looked skeptical, but waited to hear Mary's analysis.

"I don't want to make too much of this," Mary began, "but I think the Contract with America was important because it symbolized the final ideological rejection of the New Deal philosophy of the 1930s that had dominated the country right up through the 1980s. Of course, it sought to replace the New Deal with a grab-bag of ideas that had *preceded* the New Deal—ideas from the 1890s and 1920s. They were obviously inapplicable to the 1990s, but Congress didn't seem to know or care.

"For the people, though, the Contract and the truly biased 'bipartisan' policies that went with it meant that things had just gone too far. All the wealth and income in the country was being transferred to the richest people, the government and the political parties were over the edge, and something sensible and appropriate to the times just had to be done in the midst of the crisis.

"We just wanted *out* of this system, and that's when some people started talking about a new Declaration of Independence—sort of a joke at first. People laughed self-consciously, but then they started getting really serious about it. It was as if only the people remembered that this country was supposed to be a democracy and that some kind of equality and fairness was important—and the middle class just rose up and acted that way!"

"Well, I guess the important thing is that the crisis seemed to force people finally to break loose from the political parties and the system and take up the causes of problems," David summed up. "What I don't understand is why it took so long for people to see what was being done to them! It's like they had taken a pledge of eternal allegiance to the corporations, banks, financial elites, and the rest of the power structure, no matter what the cost to them!

"But I think we need a break before we tackle the second question."

We seem to be muddling through a transformation much like that of a century ago. The industrial revolution of 1877–1920 uprooted entire generations of ordinary people from their homes and livelihoods, forced them into factories and cities, and put them through prolonged hardships. Working conditions were harsh, and most were lucky to find employment that would enable their families to survive. Only a few wealthy families benefited in a permanent way—and the costs to the many were both cruel and unnecessary. Surely we can improve on that history!

The American Transformation

Much of the political transformation associated with the industrial revolution occurred *after* 1920—to be exact, in the sixteen-year stretch between 1928 and 1944. There were important political changes during the Progressive era that set the stage, but the confirmation and implementation of those ideas, institutions, and practices occurred as FDR and the New Deal grappled with the Great Depression and World War II. A new and far-reaching federal government with broad responsibilities for economic prosperity and social welfare was established in this short period. Not coincidentally, the parameters of ideas and practice established by the New Deal dominated four succeeding decades, all the way to the 1980s.

The United States is now in the midst of a similar transformation, the political impacts of which are yet to happen. The economic and social effects, however, are already clear. By comparison with other industrial nations of the world, the United States has clearly lost the economic supremacy it held for the first two or three decades after World War II. To some extent, this was inherent in the fact that other economies were rebuilt (often with American help) to the most modern standards. But it also has to do with the short-term profit orientation of U.S. corporations and investors and their resistance to taxes and long-term investment in the United States. This fact is the principal explanation for the biased effects of our transformation: essentially, the rich get much richer and the middle class and the poor get much poorer.

In rates of economic growth, the United States trails several other countries: if projections are made based on comparative growth rates for the past twenty years, the United States will be surpassed by Japan and the European Community in 2003 and will be eclipsed in another ten or twenty years. Although the United States has had a spurt of rising productivity and growth, it has been accompanied by continued decline in workers' real wages, benefits, and pensions. Such rate-of-growth comparisons, together with the income gap between rich and poor that has widened dramatically in the past two decades, lead many observers to predict Third World status for the United States by 2020.

When other criteria such as social indicators or "quality-of-life" indicators are used for comparison, the United States falls well behind other industrial nations. Social indicators and quality-of-life measures are simply not important to the bottom line of corporate profit-and-loss statements. By the UN's Development Index, for example, which adds literacy and longevity to purchasing power comparisons, the United States trails all other industrialized countries and barely matches the leading developing nations. When comparisons include infant mortality, homicide rates, or proportions of people in prisons, the United States is already deep among Third World countries. Table 2.1 reproduces some typical comparisons with other industrialized nations and paints a perhaps unwelcome picture of American circumstances.

Another major change often noted is the fact that separate national economies are giving way in certain key aspects to a single global economy. International trade has expanded so that production for export and consumption of imports are much larger shares of overall economic activity than ever before. The emergence of the global economy is related in important ways to technological developments. First, greatly improved communications technology has enabled the relocation of corporate productive facilities toward lowest-cost labor without losing control from headquarters. The production, marketing, and distribution functions of a company can be fully integrated, even though they physically take place at widely separated sites throughout the world.

Second, electronic capabilities make possible the nearly instantaneous movement of vast sums of money from one form of investment to another anywhere on the globe. Banks, currency traders, and brokerage houses can invest or speculate in bond or stock or money markets on a completely global basis.

Finally, robotization and other means of automating production have combined with faster means of transportation to facilitate lowest-cost "just in time" production and competitive sales anywhere in the world. Smaller products or multiple small components can be shipped quickly to assembly points close to available markets.

TABLE 2.1

SOCIAL INDICATORS, "BIG 7" NATIONS

	United States	Other "Big 7" nations
Birth rate of teenage women, per 100,000, ages 15 to 19, 1980–81	53	21
AIDS cases per 100,000 persons, officially reported, as of 1991	81	14
Murders per 100,000 persons, reported to police, 1988–90	9.4	3.3
Murders per 100,000 males, ages 15 to 24, 1987–88	21.9	1.4
Reported rapes, per 100,000 women, ages 15 to 59, 1980–85[a]	114	13
Prison population per 100,000 persons, 1988–90[b]	426	74
Households with handguns, by percent of all homes, 1981–83	29	4
Municipal waste annually generated, tons per capita, 1988	1,901	849
National election voters, by percent of eligible voters, 1971–88	50	78
Paid vacation days, average per year, 1991	11	24

SOURCE: Andrew L. Shapiro, *We're Number One* (New York: Vintage, 1992), passim. The "Big 7" nations are Canada, France, Italy, Japan, West Germany, the United Kingdom, and the United States.

a. Excluding West Germany
b. Excluding Canada

The principal beneficiaries of the new high-tech global economic system are the transnational corporations with the capital and single-mindedness to take advantage of the scale of the newly available opportunities. Acknowledging no national loyalties, such corporations own resources throughout the world, produce in the lowest labor-cost areas, and often dwarf and/or manipulate national governments. They are stateless in their commitment to maximum profit and their disregard for governments and people. When faced with controls or taxes, they invoke free-market ideology or the threat of capital flight or loss of business confidence to intimidate national governments.

Another vital element in this global transformation is the growing part played by the increasingly deregulated and newly aggressive financial sector. Not just banks, but also insurance companies, pension trusts, mutual funds, and a variety of brokerage houses and other investors have created new financial instruments to take advantage of speculative profit opportunities in and between the world's stock, bond, commodity, and currency markets. Such paper transactions rarely produce tangible things of value but can result in spectacular profits—or losses. Commenting on the implications of such short-term speculation, Kevin Phillips says in *Arrogant Capital,*

> [T]he impact on the real economy has been pernicious, not least in the transformation of finance from patient capital to impatient speculation.... In the world of computer programs and tailored derivative instruments, where the money goes or what it does in its brief minutes, hours, or days of electronic existence is morally meaningless: what counts—*all that counts*—is that it returns to its home screen a slightly more swollen slug of green or gray digits than it began.

Phillips's concern is that such speculative finance combined with the concentration of great wealth in the hands of a tiny elite are the mark of a great power in the late stage of its final decline. He compares the United States to Spain in the sixteenth century, Holland in the eighteenth, and Britain at the turn of the twentieth, and finds much the same processes at work.

The cumulative effect of all these changes has brought the United States to a point where individualism, self-interest, and political opportunism seem to have crowded out any sense of moral or social purpose. Crime and drug use statistics seem to confirm the decline of the work ethic and deterioration of the social fabric. Pressures for economic, sociocultural, and, most importantly, political change are reaching the point where they simply cannot be contained. The vital question is what direction this change will take—toward real solutions to appropriately defined versions of our problems or toward the variety of ideological illusions or narrowly self-interested "answers" that shape so much of our current political dialogue.

Defining the Problem

The current American problem is one integrated problem with three interdependent and equally important aspects or components—economic, political, and sociocultural. No one of these components is determinative of the others. Instead, all three function as factors that interact with the other two and together constitute the integrated core "problem," which may be quickly summarized as economic decline and income polarization, political gridlock and alienation, and sociocultural fragmentation and conflict.

The Economic Dimensions

The standard of living and quality of life in any society depend directly on how wealth and income are produced and, more important, *distributed*. In the United States, this pattern is primarily a reflection of the dynamics of the private capitalist economy and secondarily the product of what government does with respect to that economy. In recent years, the two sets of forces have combined to bring about comprehensive policy changes.

In the context of the shift to a global high-tech economy, dominant corporations and banks and the government have combined to (1) eliminate millions of good jobs, (2) make the very rich much richer and everybody else poorer, and (3) employ taxing and spending policies that put us deep in debt and prevent needed public investment in developing the economy and preserving environmental quality. Moreover, they have (4) created a climate in which we accept as inevitable a globalism and free trade that is great for transnational corporations and banks but bad for most working people. These are the four key dimensions of the economic component of our problem.

1. *The loss of good jobs for Americans in the United States.* In the industrial-era economy of the immediate postwar United States, about half the labor force was unionized and about 40 percent held good blue-collar jobs. By 1990, union membership in the private sector was below 15 percent; blue-collar jobs made up only 25 percent of the total, and many of them were at reduced wages and benefits. A few jobs were being added in the high-tech and managerial levels, but most new jobs were in services, particularly retail and fast-food services, at drastically lower wages and benefits than in manufacturing jobs. The reasons were well recognized: corporate relocation to low-wage areas of the world, automation, and lack of public and private investment in the United States, both in infrastructure and in new productive facilities.

For all these reasons, real wages in the United States have held steady or dropped for most wage earners since 1973. In addition to the collapse of the trade unions, automation, downsizing, and the shift from manufacturing to service jobs, corporations have reduced or eliminated pensions and health-care benefits and the government has reduced social services and infrastructure investments. The extent of the contrast between rising productivity and surging profits on the one hand, and the drop in workers' share of national income and stagnation of real wages on the other, was the subject of a graphic display in *Business Week* in May of 1995, under the heading, "A Startling Shift in Income Shares."

2. *The huge new income gap.* The result of all these changes has been a dramatic polarization of income in which the upper 5

percent of income-earning families, and particularly the highest 1 percent, have made huge gains in the share of all national income received. These are the people with capital to invest and/or particular advantages that enable them to profit from the new high-tech and global economy.

The entire lower 80 percent of income-earning families has experienced substantial losses in their share of national income. Hardest hit have been those in the middle, earning from $25,000 to $100,000 in 1992 dollars, many of whom have been laid off as the good blue-collar jobs have dried up. Often they are older workers who lack transferable skills and who find that new jobs are just not available even if they were to undergo retraining.

Almost totally left behind is the semipermanent underclass of poorly educated, unskilled, often mentally and physically disabled, poverty-and-welfare people. The low-paid but survival-level menial and domestic-service jobs that used to sustain some of them have left the central cities for the new high-tech suburban business areas linked to the new global economy.

The United States now has the greatest gap between rich and poor of all the industrialized nations, and the greatest in all its history. This is the single most serious economic problem we have, and it is one that pervades or overshadows every other problem we describe. Moreover, this gap is steadily growing, and current policies threaten to speed it up. Figure 2.1 compares the shares of national income received by U.S. families, ranked by earning level, between 1977 and 1989. It shows the steady decline in shares of income received by the lower four quintiles (fifths). Only the top 20 percent is increasing its share, and the middle 20 percent of all families received barely more than the top 1 percent in 1989.

3. *Fiscal policy, deficits, debt, and the failure of investment.* Since 1981, the United States—with Republicans and Democrats acting in concert—has amassed a crippling series of record-setting annual deficits and a nearly quintupled national debt. Despite incessant posturing, neither Congress nor the president seems capable of restoring fiscal sanity, protecting the value of

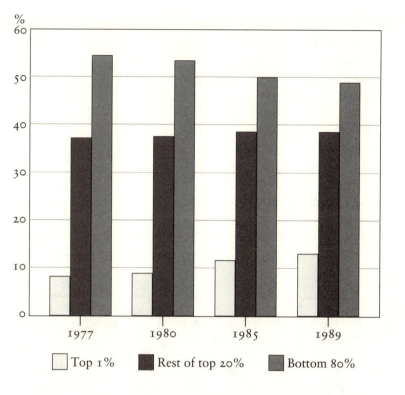

FIGURE 2.1

SHARES OF PRETAX ADJUSTED FAMILY INCOME

SOURCE: Congressional Budget Office tax simulation model, cited in *U.S. House Ways and Means Committee 1992 Green Book* (Washington, D.C.: Government Printing Office, 1992), p. 1521.

EXPLANATION: In the official data, all families are grouped by income level into segments representing 20 percent of income earners (fifths, or quintiles). The above figure collapses the lower four quintiles into "Bottom 80%" in order to contrast their earnings trends with the top 20 percent, particularly the top 1 percent. We show the top 20 percent as "Top 1%" and "Rest of top 20%" respectively. Note that the top 1 percent of families increased its share from 8.3 percent in 1977 to 13.0 percent in 1989, a gain of more than 50 percent in twelve years. See figure 3.1 (p. 61) for a projection of these trends to the year 2020.

our currency, preventing interest rates from rising, or finding ways to make long-overdue investments in public infrastructure instead of unproductive interest payments on the national debt. Former U.S. Senators Warren Rudman and Paul Tsongas summarize the situation this way:

> [S]taggering deficits continue to choke off critical public and private investment. The quality of our educational system erodes as our once-dazzling infrastructure buckles. Our nation is becoming two polarized Americas, one privileged, one poor. Our productivity grows meagerly compared to our competitors'; our savings and investment rates are a fraction of theirs. The general interest and the future are drowned out by the strident claims of

today's special interests. Even at a time when the electorate has made clear it wants change, many elected officials dare not speak the truth.

It is not so clear, of course, exactly what that "truth" really is. Often stressed as the definition of the problem is the spectacular growth of "entitlements"—such costs as pensions, Social Security, Medicare, Medicaid, unemployment benefits—that the government is committed in advance to pay to people who meet certain conditions. (These awful "entitlements" are also what the middle class has worked for and contributed payroll taxes to for fifty years.) Figure 2.2 (p. 42) presents a typical projection (assuming no change in policy) of the future growth of entitlement spending plus payment of interest on the national debt. Drawn from the *Final Report of the Bipartisan Commission on Entitlement and Tax Reform* in 1995, the figure shows that entitlements and interest will by themselves equal all federal revenues by about 2012, and entitlements alone will consume all revenues by 2030.

But at least part of this problem is also the result of the many loopholes in, and declining progressivity of, the nation's tax system. Social Security taxes are a particularly regressive component, taking 7.65 percent of the first $62,700 earned from all employees' wages, regardless of their income level. There is also the political lure and tactic of promising tax cuts, particularly for the already rich, rather than tax increases or newly progressive rates that might tap the truly rich.

The "truth" is that the problem is at least as much a revenue problem as it is an entitlement problem, as we show in detail later. Leaders must accept, and voters must take responsibility for and unflinchingly support, an entirely new approach to fiscal policy that places the long-term needs of the community above short-term self-interest on the part of corporations *and* individuals.

One of the victims of the squeeze between revenues and spending, and of the lack of political will that has resulted in huge annual deficits, is public investment. As Senators Rudman

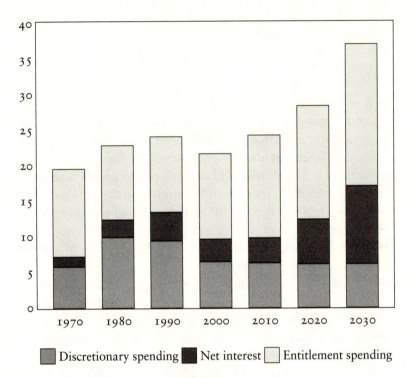

Discretionary spending █ Net interest ☐ Entitlement spending

FIGURE 2.2

FEDERAL SPENDING AS A PERCENTAGE OF GROSS
DOMESTIC PRODUCT (ACTUAL TO 1990, PROJECTIONS
UNDER CURRENT LAW TO 2030)

SOURCE: Bipartisan Commission on Entitlement and Tax Reform, *Final
Report to the President* (Washington, D.C., 1995), 9.

NOTE: Total revenues for each of these years are projected at 19 percent
of gross domestic product. That is, by 2030 revenues will not even
cover all entitlement spending.

and Tsongas stressed, we have not made the infrastructure or re-search investments crucial to maintaining a competitive econ-omy. Nor have we invested in developing human resources or in adequately protecting the environment. The latter are major fail-ures because it may be impossible to make up for either of them in the future.

4. *Globalism, free trade, and free markets.* This ideological package must be exposed as the self-serving slogan of transna-tional corporations and banks, now solemnly embedded in the recent NAFTA and GATT treaties. For decades, it has served as the cover for internationalists to serve their own ends at the cost of good jobs in the United States. It also carries an aura of inevi-tability, which can serve to justify government indifference to the loss of markets.

Free trade on a global basis does advantage the strongest transnational corporations and banks. But its supposed benefits translate far more readily into increased profits than they do into steady income for employees in the United States. And because so many of the largest corporations and banks of the world economy are no longer headquartered in the United States, the slogan may mean that we stand by helplessly while foreign com-panies, aided by their governments in a variety of ways, expand their shares of American markets. There is nothing inevitable or irresistible about globalism, free trade, or free markets. The United States is the only country in the world that takes this ide-ology so seriously; other governments serve their own interests quite openly, and at our expense.

The Political Dimensions

Many observers have taken note of at least some version of what we have defined above as the economic dimensions of the Ameri-can problem. But such problems are almost always seen in isola-tion and are not *connected* to the specific political system flaws that effectively prevent their solution. A partial exception is the work of the populist conservative Kevin Phillips, whose recent

Arrogant Capital offers a long list of modest political reforms that would make the system more responsive to voters. The failure to connect politics and economics directly in thinking and acting is itself a significant part of the American problem.

Americans have long credited the Constitution of 1787 with creating a governance system that could solve any problem and assure enduring prosperity. Americans seem collectively to have denied the need for adaptive political change, employing instead what we earlier called the "false patriotism" of insisting on the eternal validity of the status quo. That confident belief is now being put to its severest test since the Civil War. Insightful as the Founders may have been about human nature and ways of containing power, their work has simply been overtaken by changing conditions and new technology. Let us consider just a few examples.

Television is not just a visual newspaper: it creates a wholly different kind of politics and a new way of dealing with issues. It is both absolutely essential to getting elected and fabulously expensive. Similarly, special interests and lobbyists, particularly the financial system (with its capacity to unmake governments in a few days' time), have made Washington, D.C., into a political setting where power sources outside government routinely shape the actions of the people's elected representatives.

For both these reasons, big money plays a far more decisive part in governance than the Founders could ever have imagined. What the Founders worried about was the possibility that popular majorities might do hasty or ill-considered things, and so they constructed a system with multiple checks and balances and effective veto points. In this effort, the Founders were very successful; today's gridlock attests to their achievement. Although so often ignored by those who offer the most elaborate economic and social prescriptions, the political system itself is part of the problem, in at least the following major ways.

1. *The cost of television and political campaigns generally.* This is a background factor that dramatically increases the lever-

age enjoyed by big money in shaping political outcomes, and it must be addressed somehow. Candidates and would-be candidates are already totally dependent on a relative handful of available sources for the vast sums needed to mount a credible campaign. *No big money, no credible candidacy—and probably no election.*

A web of mutually reinforcing factors makes this problem almost intractable. Legislators will almost never vote to limit either their supporters' spending opportunities or their own sources of funding; the media profit greatly from abundant and unlimited political advertising and want it to continue; and the courts have held that contributing money is a form of protected free speech. Meaningful campaign finance reform is thus almost impossible to achieve. And so the cost of television political campaigns continues to rise.

2. *The power of corporations, banks, and the wealthy over Congress and the president.* If some kind of popular government is going to be preserved, the role of special interests and their financial contributions must be controlled. Through their extensive web of well-paid and well-connected lobbyists and the prospect of campaign contributions, the special interests and particularly the financial industry have acquired dominance over the people's elected representatives, both Democrats and Republicans. This dominance can be subtle or blatant; that is, elected representatives genuinely believe in and *want* to do what business desires, or they feel that they must toe the line on issues not crucial to their districts in order to remain eligible for campaign funding.

Income polarization exacerbates political inequality. As income distribution becomes more and more skewed toward the upper 5 percent and upper 1 percent, political leverage follows. Those with money can make contributions to television usage, campaigning, and lobbying; those without, cannot. The more the economy widens the income gap between rich and poor, the more political power accrues to the rich.

3. *Unresponsiveness, loss of confidence, and the shrinking electorate.* The political health of the United States (i.e., responsiveness, legitimacy, and support for government actions) is at stake. The concentration of economic power and effective domination by big business and the wealthy are undermining the U.S. claim to democracy. To be legitimate and have the ability to ask its citizens to support it, a purportedly democratic government needs to have a substantial majority of eligible voters engage in that minimal act of political participation: voting. The turnout at American presidential elections in the late nineteenth century was in the high 80 percent levels, even 90 percent at times. Now it is barely 50 percent, and in congressional years even lower. Given a political system that responds primarily to big-money contributors, but is not beyond aiding well-organized special interests that can mobilize blocs of voter support, the great bulk of ordinary citizens may accurately see the system as unresponsive to their interests. In time, their loss of confidence in this system is quite rational: it does not serve their needs and wants. Faced with unrelenting attacks on government by the wealthy and others who have no need of it—and by those who are their political servants—ordinary people may join the ranks of the disaffected and effectively withdraw from electoral participation. This is exactly what has happened: middle- and working-class people have quit voting, while the relatively affluent continue to vote—and thus acquire greater and greater weight in elections.

Table 2.2 offers a comparison of voting turnout by income level and party preference. While based on the 1988 presidential election—the last "normal" election—these have been more or less standard patterns in all elections over the past decades. The table shows that turnout increases with income and measures how much additional weight the relatively affluent gain because of this. Ironically, the lower income levels—the very people who stand to gain from government services—are the ones who have been discouraged from voting and have withdrawn from the active electorate. The pattern of preferences shows that the combination of turnout and withdrawal has substantially advantaged Republican candidates.

TABLE 2.2

VOTER TURNOUT AND PREFERENCE
BY INCOME QUINTILES, 1988

Income quintiles	Turnout	1988 vote	Democratic
Lowest	30%	10%	64%
Next lowest	38	13	54
Middle	49	21	47
Next highest	59	26	39
Highest	67	30	36

SOURCES: Sources for turnout and preference include the U.S. Bureau of the Census and the Committee for the Study of the American Electorate. These sources do not always employ the same categories and definitions, and the authors of this book have made certain extrapolations and closely bounded estimates. We are convinced that the ratios are accurate within one or two percentage points.

EXPLANATION: The table uses the same official source of income data as figure 2.2. It compares these quintiles in terms of their turnout rates, effective proportions of the 1988 electorate, and voting preferences. The percent of the 1988 vote (column 3) is the proportional weight that a quintile (20 percent of the people) would have at their turnout rate. For example, when the highest-earning 20 percent of the people turn out to vote at a rate of 67 percent and the other quintiles turn out at the rates given, the highest income earners will represent 30 percent of the actual voting electorate—or half again the weight that their numbers alone would allow them.

The Sociocultural Dimensions

The sociocultural resentments, fragmentation, and conflict that characterize the United States are as important as the economic and political dimensions of the core American problem. But the sociocultural dimensions are *different* in that they do not lend themselves to "solutions." And they appear to have both general and specific forms.

General sociocultural trends include the decline of public spiritedness and long-term concern for the future of the country's children; the loss of a sense of moral and social purpose in the absence of the Cold War; and a decline in the notion of public stewardship for natural resources and the environment. These characteristics are general to almost the entire society, with the possible exception of the very wealthy. General to the still-large middle class of Americans is the feeling that the hard-working and taxpaying middle class is being played for a sucker, with a rich governing elite using the government's tax revenues and social services to give the nonworking poor and blacks a free ride. Associated feelings include the convictions that government and other institutions cannot be trusted, politicians are corrupt, and greed and self-interest characterize the entire U.S. establishment. Towering over all these factors and giving them special urgency is the feeling of economic pressure—inability to keep up despite two incomes—and the loss of the American Dream.

Figures 2.3 and 2.4, drawn from a 1995 *Business Week/ Louis Harris* poll, document these characteristics of American attitudes. Levels of confidence in government and other institutions have fallen steadily since such polls began in the 1960s, reaching new lows almost every year. Those expressing "a great deal of confidence" in the federal government, for example, stood at 42 percent in 1966, in the early stage of the Vietnam war—and only 8 percent in 1995. Not surprisingly, the U.S. government was seen as representing special interests rather than the American people by a margin of more than two to one.

Optimism, or faith in the future, always a distinguishing American characteristic, seems to be fading. Expectations about their children having a better life than the respondents dropped

I. Faith in Institutions

"As far as people in charge of running each of the following are concerned, would you say that you have a great deal of confidence, only some confidence, or hardly any confidence at all in them?"

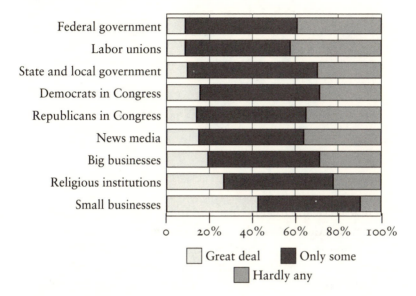

II. Who's Represented?

"In general, does the U.S. government usually represent interests of the American people or the narrow concerns of special interest groups?"

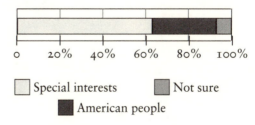

FIGURE 2.3

PUBLIC CONFIDENCE IN INSTITUTIONS, 1995

SOURCE: *Business Week*/Harris Poll, 13 March 1995.

I. Children's Prospects

"Do you expect your children will have a better life than you have had, a worse life, or a life about as good as yours?"

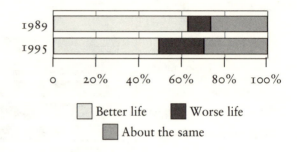

II. The American Dream: Now and in the Future

"For most Americans, do you think the American Dream of equal opportunity, personal freedom, and social mobility has become easier or harder to achieve in the past ten years?"

"And do you think this American Dream will be easier or harder to achieve in the next ten years?"

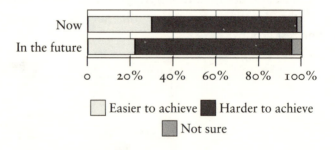

FIGURE 2.4

PUBLIC CONFIDENCE IN THE FUTURE, 1995

SOURCE: *Business Week*/Harris Poll, 13 March 1995.

by almost 25 percent between 1989 and 1995. When asked whether the American Dream was harder or easier to achieve today than ten years ago, respondents saw it as "harder" by a more than 2-to-1 ratio. By an even larger ratio, they expected it to be even harder ten years from now.

These responses are profoundly pessimistic and show graphically how deep the anxiety and insecurity of Americans run. These general feelings set the stage for the more specific tensions and conflicts that mark our times.

Specific issues often pit one culture group against another in direct confrontation. The United States is now in the midst of a genuine "culture war" in which some groups seek to assert their values or preferred beliefs and lifestyles over those of others. This is partly the natural product of significant social change accompanied by severe economic pressures in a restive, large-scale, multicultural society.

But it is also partly the manufactured product of a few political activists and ideological separatists, who seize the moment to emphasize their differences from everybody else. They often are deplored or cheered on by a much larger body of political opportunists. The latter often cynically employ culture-war symbols (race, religion, patriotism, etc.) to obscure or confuse economic and political issues so that, for example, our widening income polarization remains unrecognized and/or undisturbed.

The issues of the culture war are more value laden and less tangible than the economic or political dimensions of the American problem. At times they take the form of single issues that some assert to be paramount, such as abortion, prayer in schools, flag desecration, or rights to possess the weapons of one's choice. When such issues are indeed the main or only issues for people, they create a zero-sum game in which there are only winners or losers. Less explosive but nevertheless important cultural issues involve English as the common-denominator language, gender and racial preferences, immigration, sexual orientation, and the content of K–12 and college curriculums.

Our culture war began in the 1960s with reactions against the lifestyle changes of those years and continued with greater reactions against the Vietnam war—and even more powerfully against those who opposed the war. Governor George Wallace of Alabama eloquently expressed the resentments and frustrations of millions of Americans, and his message has been carried forward by many others. More recently, the Christian Right has escalated the level of cultural conflict, particularly with respect to abortion but also regarding prayer in schools and a variety of school curriculum issues.

While these can be major issues in their own right, most important for our purposes is the way in which sociocultural claims can obscure or redefine basic economic issues. In economic hard times, sociocultural issues are likely to be felt even more powerfully. For example, fear of foreigners and concern for immigration policy rise as lower-level jobs are reduced. Or race baiting about racial job preferences may be used to deflect attention from the fact that there are no jobs. Welfare spending, although comparatively small and directed more to white families than to black, may still be presented as the taxing of working whites for the benefit of indolent blacks.

The main point here is that sociocultural issues function both to focus complaints against other (probably equally hard-pressed) groups in the society *and* to deflect attention from more substantial issues of the society as a whole. Just because they are felt so strongly and reflect basic cleavages, they are sufficiently compelling to obscure other important issues and offer opportunities for deliberate scapegoating.

What are the goals of a problem-solving program? First, and the best that can be hoped for in the near term, is that tensions can be reduced and tolerance restored, perhaps by solving the problems that *can* be solved—restoring jobs and prosperity, providing long-term futures for young people and economic security for all, recognizing the crucial role of the environment, and renewing the vitality of our political community.

Another goal is to understand that people under a variety of economic and social pressures feel and express their anxieties and frustrations in different ways, but usually at "normal" levels. When such feelings are deliberately exacerbated for political purposes, such as by radio talk-show hosts or political extremists, the intensity with which they are expressed rises to near-hysterical levels and may result in violent acts.

Third, and most important to long-term political reconstruction, is to accomplish a combined revival and reform of the underlying values and beliefs of the society. Essentially, this requires that the middle class and its values and attitudes be revalidated. The work ethic, a sense of community, and faith in the future of the middle class have all been denied and denigrated in the past decades. Individual responsibility has been corrupted into mere self-interest, and a natural concern for economic security has been trivialized into consumerism.

A long-term perspective with the whole community in mind must eventually replace the short-term self-interest of individuals that now characterizes much of the United States. Our individualism, antigovernment bias, and free-market ideology must all be

North America Syndicate, 2/17/95

adapted to a future in which governments, once recaptured by their people, can and do perform valuable service on behalf of a community that, for example, understands its dependence on a quality environment, sensibly maintained. This is a distant goal, but the necessary dialogue needs to begin. For the moment, our reality is all that is visible, and it can seem discouraging.

THREE

Forward to the 1890s:
The Basic Scenarios

David turned to a fresh page of his notebook a little self-consciously as Jeff and Mary waited patiently for him to resume. "We're on my second question, about how you felt as things got started. For example, what gave you the confidence to do anything at all? What did you really think would result from all your efforts?"

Jeff and Mary exchanged wry smiles, and Jeff said softly and with exaggerated courtesy, "Your turn to lead off, my dear."

"Thanks a lot," Mary responded dryly.

"I don't think we had any confidence at all, David," she began. "Essentially, we were afraid of everything—of things getting worse all the time: more crime and violence, more disintegration and name-calling between groups, declining wages and rising taxes, greater and greater distance between people and whoever was running the government. We were afraid of change, afraid of the collapse of our economy and our country, and afraid of the prospect of failure if we tried to do anything about it. Things just looked hopeless. Most people were frustrated or just plain angry, and many of them had given up voting or even listening to what was going on in politics because it all seemed so irrelevant."

"Well, what happened to get things started?" David looked eagerly from Mary to Jeff, who appeared locked in his own thoughts.

"It wasn't one moment or one event, David," Jeff finally stirred. "I remember your mom and I having long conversations about how bad the future looked, and how we might cope with it by moving somewhere. Every time another new set of statistics came out about layoffs or wage decline accompanied by corporate profits setting new records, or some horrible crime by children was reported, or some absurd new tax gimmick was announced by politicians, we would think despairingly about the future.

"We finally started kind of purposefully talking with our friends about how they felt about the future, in order to get some new ideas for how to avoid what had begun to seem inevitable. You were two or three years old at the time, and most of our friends had young children also. As we listened to ourselves, and thought about you, we began to realize that there really was no escape. Either we continued to just let things happen—which clearly would mean a harsh, violent, and unpleasant life for you if you survived at all—or we had to try to do something. I think all our friends, and obviously lots more people all across the country, arrived at the same conclusion at about the same time."

Mary laughed appreciatively. "There's your confidence, David—a confidence based in desperation and fear and the sense that you have at least to try for the sake of your children or things will surely get worse. It may sound trivial, but it's a big moment when people finally give up the assumption that things will get better and finally internalize the conviction that change is instead inevitably going to make things worse. Once we all got to that point, the only question was whether to accept chaos and decline or to invest our time and energy in trying to do something about it. None of us had been active politically before. Of course we all felt powerless and afraid. Of course failure was far more likely than success."

"But you can't live your life that way," Jeff said firmly. "Particularly if you have children and hopes for them. We didn't think strategically at first. We just knew that we had to commit ourselves to what looked like a long struggle with no guarantees. It wasn't all that rational an idea at the start, either. Our early momentum came primarily from a special kind of faith, a spiritual quality that began changing us as individuals and then connected us with others and with the natural world around us and gave us hope that somehow we could find a way."

"That's true," Mary concurred. "It was not religion in any organized fashion. God knows"—Mary suppressed a giggle at using that expression—"there were certainly enough organized Christians of various kinds advocating this or that policy or program at the time. What your dad is talking about is an inner sense of human connectedness and unity with nature that gives rise to a sense of infinite possibilities and choices, if only you trust yourself and others and act to bring about your goals. Not to make too much of this, of course," Mary returned to her usual objectivity, "but it really helped to give us a sense of purpose and possibility at the start."

"Yes," Jeff said soberly. "It helped bring our chances up to a tolerable one in ten. But we always knew that other results were far more likely than that we would succeed."

"What did you really expect to happen, Dad?" David looked up from his notebook inquiringly.

"Oh, a continuing spiral of decline and a constantly worsening crisis—probably ending up in either an actual breakup of the United States or a kind of authoritarian 'Government of National Emergency' that would hold things together by force. We thought of it then as the United States becoming a Third World country, in the sense that a tiny elite enjoyed nearly all the wealth and power of the country and isolated itself from everybody else. The military and the police would protect the elite and maintain some kind of order among the people, whose lives would be harsh, lawless, and violent—I should have said nasty, brutish, and short," he added quickly.

Mary picked up Jeff's litany. "And then there was always the prospect of small wars or massive terrorism. Or perhaps one of the old parties—Democrat or Republican, it didn't matter—would go lurching off in search of a new New Deal or an old Square Deal or something, and speed up the process of becoming a Third World country. Practically every candidate tried to whip up racial or religious or ethnic antagonisms, and we could only see that kind of politics getting worse and resulting in riots and other kinds of violence."

David looked back in his notebook for a question he had jotted down. "Did anybody see your movement as another attempt to save capitalism from itself?"

Both Mary and Jeff erupted in laughter.

"Certainly not then," Jeff responded. "That would have been far too pretentious for anybody at the time. Besides, the problems we saw were political and cultural as well as economic. I think that while we challenged a lot of long-standing values and institutions, we always assumed that our economic system would be privately owned in the way it was in the 1990s. We just wanted it to work for hard-working middle Americans. And we wanted a political system that would be genuinely democratic and under our control."

Mary added quickly, "We had very few grand thoughts at the outset, David. All we wanted was to avoid the worst of the futures we could see in the making, by finding alternatives that people could rally around and support. It was after we realized that we *had* the potential to change things that we began to develop strategies and programs. But that discussion will have to wait until tomorrow, or all your friends will think you have abandoned them."

"Right, Mom," David agreed. "I'm running late, but this is really interesting. Thank you both," he said sincerely. "I'll be looking forward to individual sessions with each of you tomorrow morning."

When David left, Mary turned to Jeff with a smile. "Well, do you feel like a dinosaur?"

"Hell, no," Jeff laughed. "I'm getting into it! Those were exciting years, remember?"

"Yes, they certainly were." Mary nodded. "But it's hard to recapture the sense of risk and uncertainty of those days from where we are now." She laughed as she voice-commanded the television on. "Maybe I can order up a documentary from the 1990s."

I n this chapter, we show what lies ahead for the United States if middle Americans do not take matters in their own hands and redirect the country. In effect, we are describing the American futures that are consistent with the present structure of things and current trends. While likely, given the forces now in motion, these futures are certainly not inevitable *unless middle Americans allow them to be.* But one or another of them—or something much like them—will come into being if there is no assertive roar from the middle class to prevent it.

We are not making specific predictions but merely extending trend lines established over the past sixteen years for the next period of the same length, that is, to about 2012. In general, our survey follows the same three dimensions of the American problem employed in chapter 2: economic, political, and sociocultural.

U.S.A. 2012: The Basic Scenario

The Economic Problems

Continued downsizing of corporate workforces, with equivalent improvement in the bottom line of corporate profits, is inherent in the changing character of the economy. Continued wage stagnation and decline are built into the steady shift toward service occupations. More rewarding high-tech jobs will be developed, but not necessarily in the United States. In its lyrical 1994 special issue entitled "21st Century Capitalism," *Business Week* warns that the explosion of high-tech education, particularly in Asia, threatens U.S. workers even at the high end of the scale:

What makes Third World brainpower so attractive is price. A good computer circuit-board designer in California, for example, can pull down $60,000 to $100,000 a year. Taiwan is glutted with equally qualified engineers earning around $25,000. In India or China, you can get top-level talent, probably with a Ph.D., for less than $10,000.

The coming generations of American college graduates thus face real challenges in regard to the better job opportunities. High school graduates are in for even greater difficulties. But the American educational system is doing worse in preparing young people all the time, and there are few serious skill-development programs linked to employment opportunities. Without major efforts to upgrade the U.S. workforce, American workers of all ages will fall farther and farther behind in income prospects.

The continuing decline in job quality and wages in the U.S. economy contributes to the shrinkage in middle-class shares of national income. But in this case, the tax policy established over the past decades is also a major factor in redistributing wealth to the richest 1 percent and 5 percent. Every mention of tax policy for the future promises new ways of enriching the rich even faster. Proposals include cutting or eliminating capital gains taxes, a flat tax or a national sales tax, higher payroll taxes to "save" Medicare or Social Security, and, most effective of all to make the rich richer and everybody else poorer, the elimination of the progressive income tax.

Continuation of existing trends, even without new boosts from changes in tax policy, will result in greater and greater concentration of wealth at the top. Figure 3.1 reproduces the 1977–89 income data from figure 2.2 and projects the steady trend lines of those years into the near future, assuming no change in government policies. *By 2020, the top 20 percent of families will receive more than two-thirds of all national income, while the lowest 80 percent of all families will receive less than 33 percent!* The top 1 percent of families constitute a tiny but truly superrich apex of the income pyramid, having more than 27 percent of all national income.

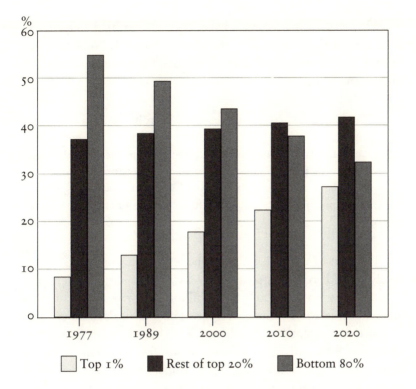

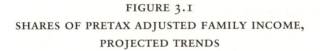

FIGURE 3.1

SHARES OF PRETAX ADJUSTED FAMILY INCOME,
PROJECTED TRENDS

SOURCE: Congressional Budget Office tax simulation model, cited in
U.S. House Ways and Means Committee 1992 Green Book (Washington, D.C.: Government Printing Office, 1992), p. 1521.

EXPLANATION: This figure extends the trends of figure 2.1 to the year
2020. Policy continuity and the 1990s data make these trends reasonable prospects. By 2020, the same top 1 percent of families will have
27.1 percent of all national income—a doubling of their 1989 share.
The terms of the Contract with America and associated tax proposals
would accelerate this change.

Looking at such prospects, Edward Luttwak entitled a chapter in a recent work "When Will the United States Become a Third World Country?"—and concluded that 2020 was about the right year. At the end of the chapter, he writes:

> [T]he political consequences can hardly fail to be catastrophic.... It would be too much to expect that democratic governance would long survive the impoverishment of all Americans except for a minority of fortunate inheritors, talented professionals, brilliant or merely lucky businesspeople, 700,000 often rapacious lawyers, and a few cunning financial manipulators.

The out-of-control federal budget, with looming deficits likely to add to the current nearly $5 trillion national debt at a rate of between $150 and $300 billion per year, poses another major threat to economic viability and political stability. This crisis is persistently defined, by Republicans and Democrats alike, as a spending problem—a problem of "entitlements" —which to be sure it is. But it is not *just* a spending problem: it is equally a revenue problem, particularly with respect to who pays what shares of their income to support the federal, state, and local governments of the country.

If current trends continue, however, we shall see further cuts in spending for the principal benefit of middle and lower classes, including cuts in entitlements that middle-class people have counted on for years. Tax increases on those most able to pay, the corporations and the wealthy, will not be considered; instead, tax cuts will be offered to them, with tax increases for the middle class needed to make up the difference. The share of national government spending devoted to paying interest on the growing deficits and debt will steadily rise, further implementing the transfer of wealth from average taxpayers to the wealthy holders of Treasury bonds.

The furor in Washington over balancing the budget is mostly a smokescreen for the actions just described—and for passing political liabilities and the resulting fallout from unmet needs to the states. There *will* be cuts; there *will not* be fairness. The burden of balancing will be borne by the middle class, while the really rich revel in the success of their political servants. And this is only the beginning: two other factors will add significantly to the growing economic problems of the middle class and the country.

One of these is the prospect that economic viability, let alone growth, may be incompatible with life-sustaining environmental quality. The ecosphere, once fundamentally damaged, cannot replenish itself. The more we use up resources, eliminate species, multiply populations, generate pollution, and tear open holes in the biosphere, the more we call into question and limit our own futures.

But methods of calculating costs and benefits in the corporate world do not value life-sustaining qualities of the environment. The call for growth is only rarely associated with the criterion of sustainability. More often, short-term growth is advocated at the cost of long-term considerations—and the inevitable result is continued environmental degradation. At some point, we will be unable to drink the water or breathe the air.

The other factor is the prospect of serious recession or even depression, perhaps accompanied by a credit or monetary collapse. In addition to widespread unemployment and hardship, this could mean a vast increase in the federal deficit: tax revenues would fall sharply, and entitlement to unemployment insurance payments and welfare would rise precipitously. The result would be a serious worsening of the federal deficit situation at the same time that people's needs for assistance were more and more compelling. This would be the precipitating crisis, with chaos and uncertainty, from which dangerous alternatives might flow.

Moreover, sources for refinancing the increased federal debt are not as readily available as they once were. Japanese money, the primary source carrying the 1981–82 debt, is no longer available. No replacement source has yet surfaced to enable the United States to continue to borrow. Ruinous interest rates will be triggered by the compelling need to borrow on the part of the nation's leading debtor. All other needs for credit will be crowded out. At the same time, trade deficits and current-account deficits vie with each other in setting new records every year. The result can only be a sharp drop in the value of the dollar and a major inflationary surge. Either way, the middle class is caught in a vicious squeeze, and its standard of living spirals farther downward.

The Political Problems

With vastly increased polarization of wealth and income comes similarly heightened political inequality. It is simply not possible to maintain that the vote of each person is of equal weight voters' economic assets differ so radically. The preservation and enhancement of the wealth of those at the top become major goals of politics and government. If campaign costs (principally for television) continue to rise at recent rates, senatorial elections in many states will reach total costs nearing $50 million and presidential elections will approach $500 million by 2012. Only the truly wealthy can be relevant to candidates and would-be candidates under such circumstances.

Faced with such compelling financial reality, what political role will remain for the ordinary citizen? He or she is effectively excluded from the choice of who will become a candidate because big money will have determined the top two or three contenders. What the candidates will do when in office will be determined by their previous contributors and/or the sources from which they can raise the campaign funding for their next election. Clearly, the linkage between citizens and "their" representatives will be even weaker than it is now, and the reasons for voting even harder to find. With any reasonable cost-benefit calculus for the time spent in becoming knowledgeable and casting a vote, the rational citizen will find any number of more rewarding things to do.

Term limits, even if achieved through a constitutional amendment, seem to offer little promise in the face of the financial realities of campaign contributions, and effective campaign finance reform is not on anybody's agenda. Indeed, the current prospect is for the elimination of all public funding for national elections so that the wealthy will have even greater influence. Citizens cannot be unaware of the fact that they are being effectively excluded: how will they feel and act?

Most likely is a steadily growing disengagement from the established political order and from traditional forms of participation. The proportion of eligible citizens actually voting will drop from its present roughly 50 percent level in presidential years, resulting in a steadily shrinking electorate of the relatively affluent and a few diehards. Citizens' identification with their government will decline still further, and the level of support for government actions will be minimal. Likely also is heightened resentment against government and politicians and contempt for their actions, particularly taxes. "Democracy" will be perceived as a charade, and with it respect for law and due process. Citizenship itself will begin to seem meaningless, and people will begin to lose their sense of self-worth. Raw power will be recognized as the reality behind social order. Effective defiance of the United States and wanton brutality against Americans by renegade regimes or terrorist bands will add to citizens' sense of helplessness and self-contempt.

In this context, the range of possibilities widens substantially. Armed bands of co-thinkers of every persuasion are likely to assert jurisdiction over various small enclaves in a search for survival and satisfaction. Notions of a national law-and-order system will give way to many particularized systems, often based on religious or ideological principles. Clashes between sects, and between sects and state or federal forces, are quite likely.

As the situation worsens, governing elites will seek to consolidate what sense of legitimacy remains among Americans for their national government by proclaiming a national emergency. To counter the growing anarchy, they will assert the need to suspend elections entirely and conduct the nation's business in an authoritarian manner. The president and an executive committee from Congress might be empowered to govern "temporarily," with the military deployed to maintain order in the country.

This is not a far-fetched scenario. Maintenance of the American economy and necessary political stability is too important for ruling elites to allow disintegration to proceed too far. There have always been contingency plans for suspending elections and/or ruling through a "Government of National Emergency" in which the military play a prominent role in maintaining order.

The question is whether ordinary citizens can be expected to remain quiescent forever in the face of drastic income polarization, dramatic downward spiraling of their standard of living, patent exclusion from effective political roles, and denigration of their values and capabilities. At least, many people will be tempted to take matters in their own hands and try to preserve what they can before it is all gone. The Third World is full of illustrations of various stages of lawlessness and piracy by armed bands, whether their origins be tribal, racial, religious, or ideological.

The Sociocultural Problems

There is a growing crisis at the soul of American society and culture. It is more than a malaise, more than a lack of shared social purpose—it is a crisis of values, trust, and self-confidence. Things just do not seem to work anymore, and the future looks even worse.

All the facts of our transformation and our economic, political, and sociocultural problems are well known to most Americans, if only viscerally or intuitively. As they have been internalized, however, they have been converted into a grim forecast —in some respects more pessimistic than the facts, bad as they are, would appear to justify. People have been made to feel that their values are no longer valid and that they are incapable of self-government—and they have begun to believe that this is true.

The sources of our spreading sense of despair and foreboding are not hard to find. One is the helplessness and frustration that one feels with respect to the entire younger generation, but particularly one's own children. Figure 3.2 compares the incomes of young (under-thirty) men in two periods, 1977–88 and 1989–92. In every case, the younger group did less well than its predecessors. A similar trend in social mobility is evident between 1967 and 1979 and 1980 and 1991: the poor are more likely to stay poor and the affluent to stay affluent than used to be the case. Not surprisingly, the proportion of middle-class people dropping into the level of the poor has also reversed and is now weighted downward. If these trends are projected into the future, we have more evidence of tightening prospects for each new generation.

As opportunities shrink and require more specialized education, the failures of the educational system become more obvious. The United States spends more by far to educate its children than other countries, but the results of testing in various subjects always favor the others. Violence among teenagers is rising rapidly, as is the suicide rate. The number of juvenile gang killings has jumped 600 percent in the past ten years and project to a truly frightening future. No doubt some bright, strongly moti-

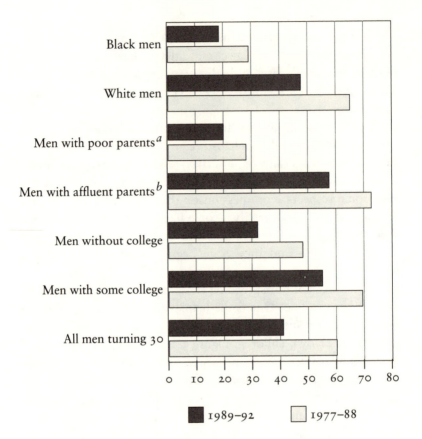

FIGURE 3.2

INCOME (SOCIAL) MOBILITY BY TIME PERIODS

Percentage of men who had earned a middle-class income
($23,042) in 1993 dollars before turning 30,
in 1977–88 and 1989–92

SOURCE: *New York Times,* 4 June 1995, E4, citing data from Greg
Duncan, Northwestern University.

a. Income less than 1.5 × poverty line.
b. Income 4 or more × poverty line.

vated, and/or lucky young people will still find ways to live happy and productive lives, but it will be far more difficult on the average than it was for today's adults.

Another source is what Americans define as the leading problem in the country: crime. Although most crime rates have dipped slightly in recent years, the public feels, by a ratio of 89 percent to 7 percent, that the crime problem is getting worse. The rate of violent crime is clearly up: there were 520 violent crimes per 100,000 population in 1985, but 750 in 1993. Assuming this basic trend line continues, the ratio will be about 1,200 by 2012. Moreover, violent crimes are far more random than previously and are thus less likely to be solved; murder is the leading example.

The future will probably show even steeper rates of increase than violent crime trends suggest because juveniles are distinctively violence prone. According to the FBI, juvenile arrests for violent crime rose 68 percent between 1984 and 1993. The U.S. attorney general says, "Never in our history have we seen this phenomenon of youth violence as random and as inexplicable." As these youth age, they will take their criminal propensities with them.

Nor does the recent binge of prison building and stiffer sentencing appear to have deterred violent crime. In 1980, our state and federal prisons held about 250,000 convicts; in 1996, the total is more than 900,000. If this rate of increase continues for another 16 years, the total will be more than 1.5 million—by far the largest number and ratio of any country in the world.

At least some part of the violent crime surge has its roots in our economic decline. Bank robberies are one example. There were about 2,000 per year in the 1970s, 3,000 per year in the early 1980s, and an average of more than 9,000 per year in the 1990s. This phenomenal 300 percent increase is the more striking because the typical robbery nets only about $2,500, and three out of every four robbers are caught and convicted. For the most part, the new robbers appear to be unsophisticated but desperate middle-class people with a need for ready cash to pay mortgages or student loans!

Paralleling rising crime rates and undoubtedly connected as well are the discouraging figures about the dysfunctions of American families. In 1992, 15 percent of all American children under eighteen lived below the poverty line, and 30 percent of all children lived in single-parent households. The rate of births out of wedlock is rising rapidly, and not primarily for teenagers: women of all races in their early twenties show the highest rate of childbearing while single. Projecting the steep rates of increase in single-parent households in the past 16 years suggests that, by 2012, 40 percent of white children and 89 percent of black children could be living in single-parent households. Nor is there any cure to be expected from so-called intact families: rates of domestic abuse and child abuse also jumped sharply in the past fifteen years.

Surveying the state of American society and culture through data such as these, *Time* characterized it in January 1995 as "the accumulated wreckage of political paralysis, endemic violence, disintegrating families, two decades of wage stagnation and cultural vertigo." While it is understandable that various religious groups such as those represented in the Christian Coalition should seek to deal with this crisis, for example, through their "Contract with the American Family," the situation is far too complex for any simple solution. *It can be addressed effectively only by a truly multidimensional approach—economic, political, and sociocultural—that is grounded in renewed social and personal responsibility and sustained, confidence-building social action by the people themselves.* Nothing else will do. But no major source proposes to do such things. Instead, both major parties would speed up the process of achieving Third World status—each in its own characteristic way, of course.

The Republican Alternative:
A High-Tech 1896

What if the Republicans controlled both the presidency and Congress for eight years or so? What changes would they make, and what would the United States be like? Essentially, it would be a high-tech version of 1896: a national government internally puny but externally bellicose, a shredded and privatized social safety net, a sharply polarized income stratification (in which the wealthy are protected by the tax system and security forces from either responsibility for or knowledge of the other 95 percent of the population), racial and ethnic scapegoating, and an overwhelming embrace of religious fundamentalism and jingoistic patriotism.

The Republican Party of 1996 consists of three contending factions, each with distinctive values and goals. The libertarians blame government for all problems and want to roll back the state to the happy "hands off" days of the 1890s and then go about their private affairs. More traditional conservatives see multiple uses for government, particularly in protecting property and investments and maintaining order, but insist that it be a fiscally conservative government controlled by responsible elites. The newest faction is made up of the social and cultural ideologues of populist conservatism and the Christian Coalition, who see themselves locked in a culture war requiring the capture and redirection of the national government to serve their ends.

Currently, the three factions are held together by the artful Republican balanced-budget focus, although they could fly apart at any time if one of them forces its values and beliefs too strongly on the others. All are represented in the Contract with America, and its successor, *Restoring the Dream: The Bold New Plan by House Republicans*. This is a comprehensive document that presents the House Republicans' plan for balancing the budget by 2002, and with it a set of policy changes that will strictly limit the role of the national government and thereby (they believe) restore prosperity. If Republicans hold power, this is where their priorities can be found.

To begin with, the Republican program acknowledges no sources of problems whatsoever except for the policies and bureaucracy of the national government. Some economic forces are recognized to be at work, such as globalization and many new forms of information-age technology, but these are exclusively opportunity producers and have no downsides. For example,

American corporations are lauded for cutting their workforces, and this "achievement" is offered as the model for government.

Although the Reagan-era tax cuts were integral to ballooning the debt in those years, the Republican program proposes $300 billion more in "family and economic growth tax cuts," offset by vastly greater proposed spending cuts. (In order to balance the budget *and* provide tax cuts, of course, there must be truly massive spending cuts—or we will experience a "Voodoo II" replay of the deficit binge of the Reagan-Bush years.)

The cuts that Republicans propose are, as they argue, actually only reductions in expected increases. *But it must be a $1.2 trillion reduction* in anticipated spending, most of which is anticipated because of the aging of the baby-boom generation and rising health-care costs.

How can spending cuts of this magnitude be made? A large number of ideological targets are available: foreign aid, support for the arts, public welfare (particularly Aid to Families with Dependent Children, or AFDC), supplemental security insurance, the departments of energy and education, support for basic research, and the ever-popular "waste, fraud, and abuse." But all these added together are still a tiny portion of the federal budget. Social Security, Medicare, defense, interest on the national debt, and Medicaid constitute the great bulk of spending, and no significant reductions can be accomplished without addressing these programs.

The Republican strategy is to "promote economic growth, expand choice, and rely on market solutions." Their proposed program first stresses the happy implications of increasing future economic growth by one percentage point over the Clinton estimates (estimates already challenged as too optimistic by many economists.) The means of doing so are of course deregulation and tax cuts. Helpfully, this takes care of half the federal spending cuts that otherwise would have to be made.

How will this additional economic growth be achieved? The Republican program expects to achieve it by instituting a simplified flat-tax approach to income taxation or by replacing the income tax entirely with a national sales tax. Under the flat tax (17 percent on all, with substantial personal allowances that take the poorest off the tax rolls), all families would pay tax at the same rate regardless of income level. Under the sales tax, families would pay the same rate on all consumption expenses. In neither case would there be any taxes on income from savings, investments, or capital gains.

These changes are expected to unleash entrepreneurial energies and save millions of unproductive hours of tax preparation—enabling the elimination of the IRS as well. That such tax changes will also be profoundly biased against low- and middle-income people, and vastly advantageous to the rich, is not mentioned. (Treasury Department estimates show 52 percent of the benefits of the proposed tax cuts going to the less than 20 percent of families earning more than $100,000 per year.)

Much stress is put on the "opportunity society" that awaits widespread use of high technology in the innovative free market. How people acquire the skills necessary to take advantage of such opportunities is also left to the free market, inasmuch as government support for education, research, and retraining is drastically reduced.

Despite the anticipated surge of economic growth from tax policy changes, massive cuts will still have to be made. Here is where the Christian Coalition finds expression. The leading candidate is the welfare system, and the central problem is identified as illegitimacy and single-parent families. Welfare is seen as the destroyer of families because it provides support for single women with children. Citing "an illegitimacy rate of 22 percent for whites and 68 percent for blacks," the document goes on to declare that "we are on the socially suicidal path of becoming a nation of dysfunctional families." The solution is twofold: prohibit welfare to unwed mothers under eighteen, and deny support for children born out of wedlock to mothers already on welfare. (The subject of abortion is not discussed.)

The Republicans also discover that since the 1950s the tax burden has somehow been shifted to middle- and lower-income people. Inflation, Democrats, and a greedy federal government share the blame—but deliberate bipartisan tax policy is discreetly ignored. The solution, however, is the proposed $500 tax credit per child, which will indeed provide some relief, but at the cost of many other tax benefits for the rich that will ultimately lead to their traditional net advantage.

The welfare and tax-credit provisions, together with a bundle of shopworn solutions such as school vouchers, privatization of various functions, sale of federal assets, and shifting responsibilities to the states, complete the Republican program. Not addressed are the five big objects of expenditures identified earlier, which must be cut drastically if the budget is to be balanced while tax cuts are implemented. Interest on the debt must be paid, and defense is actually slated for modest increments, meaning that there will need to be some unspecified but dramatic reductions in Social Security, Medicare, and Medicaid—or else another round of Reagan and Bush-style deficits and debt expansion.

Thus, against the background of drift, decline, and disintegration that is the current American prospect, the Republican program would sharpen the class differences in the country but also offer a racial/religious loincloth to obscure it for a while. Blacks, and to a lesser extent other minorities, could again be legitimate targets of resentment and ridicule. The more fundamentalist Christian denominations could happily marginalize Catholics, Jews, agnostics, and adherents of "foreign" religions. Perhaps most important, all these feelings could be subsumed in a massive surge of patriotic endorsement for a supposed "American Way"—symbolized by millions of tiny American flags, just as in the McKinley campaign of 1896.

The Democratic Alternative: Mirrors, Followed by Smoke

The American two-party system assures the possibility of a Democratic return to power. The voters' only means of expressing rejection of the government or the incumbent party under a two-party system is to vote for the "other" party. The two-party system thus enables voters either to *ratify* the actions of the party in power or to *reject* that party (or the government itself), but not necessarily to empower people or parties representing preferred alternatives to what is happening.

What, if anything, will the Democrats stand for, and how can we know? The basic split in the party, evident since the late 1970s and widening steadily throughout the 1980s, offers the best clues. The majority position, illustrated by the Democratic Leadership Council, the Clinton campaign of 1992, and the post–1995 Clinton posture, is essentially a centrist mirror of the Republicans' budget-balancing package accompanied by a heavy dose of globalism and free trade. Support for this position comes from the internationalist elites at the heart of the party's funding sources, most of its professional politicians and cultural icons, and most of its remaining trade union adherents. This majority remains firmly in control of the party machinery, particularly the presidential nominating process, and would be the beneficiary of any return to power as a result of Republican rejection.

The minority view is the leftover 1960s Great Society liberalism of feminists and liberal professionals, supported by the poor and minorities, particularly blacks, and some public-sector trade unions. It is illustrated by the various candidacies of the Reverend Jesse Jackson and a cadre of representatives in the House organized as the Congressional Black Caucus and the even smaller Progressive Caucus. For years, this band of self-styled "progressives" has sought to move the party in its direction without success. By its efforts, it succeeded only in driving relatively conservative Democrats toward the Republicans and enabling the latter to paint the Democrats as affirmative action "liberals." To win elections, this alternative would have to mobilize millions of poor and alienated nonvoters, a massive and unlikely enterprise.

The centrist Democrats represented by the early-and-late Bill Clinton are committed to budget balancing on a slower timetable, but with essentially the same mix of reductions in entitlements and "middle-class" tax cuts. In domestic policy, they would offer in effect a mirror of the Republican programs, although with less ideological fervor. Congressional Democrats, effectively isolated by the Clinton budget posture, have the option of becoming irrelevant mirrors or invisible opponents of the Republicans-Clintons. The Black Caucus and the Progressive Caucus, for example, submitted in May 1995 an interesting proposal for balancing the budget by 2002 that cut defense, raised corporate taxes, and maintained entitlements—all to complete media and public invisibility.

In foreign policy, the centrist Democrats do have a strong commitment and would have a significant impact on the general pattern of drift, decline, and disintegration. Under the smoke cloud of globalism, free trade, and free markets, they would speed up the process of giving away American jobs and enabling foreign exporters to dominate our markets. The transnational corporations and banks would gain, and everybody else would lose, from more arrangements such as NAFTA and GATT. As long as other countries manage their trade policies to maintain production and full employment at home and maximum exports abroad, the United States only wounds itself by facilitating corporate flight and welcoming cheap imports. Ronald Steel, writing in the *Washington Post National Weekly*, sums up this problem very neatly:

> A nation that is unwilling or unable to protect its own workers because it is shackled to such intellectual abstractions as open markets and the unrestricted export of money and jobs, is a nation doomed to internal strife and second class status. An enlightened American nationalism ... will also stop providing free military protection for its economic rivals in order to maintain the illusion that it thereby preserves its status as a "superpower." There is a more accurate description for that role: unpaid security guard.

Forward to the 1890s

If the Democrats return to power, therefore, we can expect only a mirror of Republican programs or the smoke cloud of globalism—and in neither case will the basic pattern of drift, decline, and disintegration be altered. The basic scenario, and the two parties' alternatives, all flow in the same direction, although at different speeds. In social and economic and political terms, we are headed for the 1890s.

Two major independent observers have recently noted the parallels between our times and the 1890s. Writing in *U.S. News and World Report* in November 1994, the political analyst Michael Barone argued that the nature of the divisions between parties and cultural groups in the United States, and the dynamics between classes, resembled 1896 more than the recent past. As in 1896, neither party addresses the real problems of the country, substituting either false patriotism or racial and culture-war diversion.

More globally oriented was the argument in the *New York Times Magazine* in June 1995 ("Forward to the Past") to the effect that, all across the world, nationalism is rising as nation-states decline and "the future is starting to look like the past; the 1990s are starting to look like the 1890s." After a series of telling comparisons, including noting that the 1890s were a time of "disruptive booms and crashes, and of prolonged economic stagnation and depression," author Walter Russell Mead concludes:

> Before long, some of the structures now being carted away will be rebuilt in haste when we rediscover the virtues of national governments strong enough to protect both individuals and nations from the ravages of economic and social catastrophe.

The Essential Agenda

Any viable program to solve the problems of the American middle class today must change the structure of power in the United States—replacing the current dominance of corporate and wealthy elites and their political parties with direct middle-class control. The way to do this is to take on three key problems or trends that are now implacably constructing a Third World future for the United States. None of them is addressed by the Republican or Democratic Party, or for that matter by any of the major contemporary prescriptions for "renewing" or "rethinking" or "creating a new civilization" for America. (Nor do any of these prescriptions challenge the current *structure of power* in the country in any way. The three key problems are:

1. Wealth and income are being redistributed from the middle classes to the top 1 percent or at most 5 percent, and the United States—already with the greatest income inequality of any industrialized nation—is growing more top-heavy every day. Changing patterns of jobs, wages, and taxes all contribute to this surge and are making for a tiny dominant elite atop the social pyramid.

2. The same elite and its political servants dominate the structure of power in the American political system, using their financial resources to control both major political parties and to shape the general public understanding of issues and events. The chief beneficiaries are the transnational corporations and banks and the very wealthy, and to some extent the professional classes that help them manage the society. This inequality and domination mock the rhetoric of democracy that is still heard when the people are blamed for the conditions and problems of the country.

3. The values and capabilities of the middle class are denied and derided, as if in justification for putting greater distance between the people and their government. We are moving from an outmoded and unworkable representative system to a transparently manipulative system in which the people have even less control. Citizens' capabilities have been denied, and their desires frustrated, for so long that they have turned their attention elsewhere—increasingly leaving the field to the corporate-financial elite and the special interest scramble.

There is one ray of hope that should be identified before we proceed to outline the vision and program of a middle-class revolution that *can* solve these problems. Both major parties may simply break up, as their major factions insist on getting their own way and the voters continue the trend toward independent parties and candidates. The two wings of the Democratic Party have little in common except memory. The Republicans' three factions, as noted, are held together by the existence of the Democrats and the artful government-dismantling program in which the goals of all are represented. The catalyst of the breakup of both parties could be an independent party or candidate of stature or a major reform program such as we now describe.

Part II

The Middle-Class Revolution

FOUR

An Economy for Americans — All Americans

Balanced unsteadily on a kitchen stool, David nursed his third cup of coffee and idly ran the day's sports schedule on the interactive television. Although it was not yet 10 A.M., Mary had been on the phone for the past half hour, talking with her mother. Now in her late seventies, Mary's mother was a real survivor, cheerful and busy despite the struggles of making ends meet for twenty years after the death of her husband. Mary's father, laid off from the automobile plant in his fifties and denied his pension, had gone through long periods of unemployment until his pride finally collapsed into alcoholism and eventually death. Mary kept in regular touch with her mother, and always telephoned on holidays. She finally closed down the phone system and looked up.

"I hope you didn't mind that I got you up early, David," she said, "but I wanted to be sure we got started on the economic program, the most important component of the changes."

"It's okay, Mom, you only beat my alarm by ten minutes. I cut back to only two reunions last night just so we could put in some time this morning. But what makes you so emphatic about the economic program as the most important?"

Mary leaned back in her chair, put her feet up on the lower

rung of David's stool, and frowned slightly in concentration. "The economy's always paramount, David. Nothing is as important to people as jobs and income. When times are tough, economic issues take precedence over everything else. In the 1990s, people had been through twenty years of hard times and it looked like thirty more were ahead. Many folks had just lost hope for the future, for themselves and, more important, for their children and even grandchildren. When the economy collapsed a few years later, no one was surprised."

"But what about all the other things that people fought about in the nineties, Mom, like racial and gender and religious issues?" David asked.

Mary shifted impatiently. "Red herrings, mostly," she replied. "Used by opportunistic politicians to divert people from understanding the way that the economy worked almost entirely for the really rich." Mary was getting warmed up, and David was beginning to understand why she was such an effective advocate, in court and in negotiations.

"Besides," she went on, "economics involves tangible results, things people can see, food on the table, work and income. You have to offer that kind of results if you want people to pay attention and join you in a social movement. And you have to have a *program*, some specific justifiable and tangible goals and policies that you want to produce, in order to mobilize people. You can't fight something, particularly the status quo, with nothing. You have to have something specific to put in its place that people can believe in and that they think will be better."

"But, Mom, how did you and the others happen to come up with so many new ideas all at once, and what made them believable to so many voters?"

Mary jumped to her feet and stood over David. "There was nothing new about our program at all, nothing far-fetched or magical. Everything we proposed had been around for years, except for the system we developed for putting all major issues under the direct control of the voters. Once we had that in place, it broke everything else open. Essentially, we took back control of the government from the corporations and banks and their bought-and-paid-for politicos and enacted a comprehensive economic nationalist program. We created good jobs, closed that incredible income gap between rich and poor, and restored security for the future. Remember your tag line last night about saving capitalism from itself? We didn't just *save* it, we *humanized* it! Of course, that last part isn't assured yet," Mary ended more quietly.

David was determined to press for more detail. "Well, what made voters believe in that program all of a sudden? I thought the conservatives had chased you liberals all the way back to your ivory towers!"

Mary smiled patiently and declined the bait. "Our program was way beyond liberalism *and* conservatism, and you know it. It wasn't a synthesis, either, but rather a kind of transcending of all the outdated ideologies. We started with what we all shared and needed as a community for the long term, and joined in discouraging one another from falling back into what set us apart as groups or special interests or what we wanted as selfish individuals.

"In other words, we thought nationally while we acted locally *and* nationally at the same time." Mary smiled wryly at her revision of the old slogan. "And we were frank about the purposeful use of *our* government to fulfill *our* shared needs. We knew that we needed to encourage investment in preserving and developing resources, including both people and the environment, and that we had to encourage and reward innovation of various kinds. We were practical *and* visionary," Mary concluded proudly, "and it seems to be still working today."

"Yes, it does," David said somewhat grudgingly. "But have you really answered my question about why it became possible at that particular moment in history? I'm sorry if I sound a little professorial here, but there seems to be something missing."

"You sound like a *prosecutor*," Mary said grimly, but with acceptance. "Maybe I have to borrow some of your father's emphasis on spirituality and faith to give you an adequate answer, but here goes. I think people just got to the point where they had had it with ideology, separatism, self-interest, me-first, and political posturing. The middle class was just plain angry, David. Those motivations weren't getting anybody anywhere, except that the really rich were getting really richer and 90 percent of us—*90 percent!*—were getting poorer.

"Something just had to be done, *urgently,* and that meant *together, cooperatively,* as is always the case in times of real danger. Our obviously shared dependence on a sustainable environment certainly helped. It's humbling when you think of humanity as just one species, and dependent on all the unknowable aspects of nature to stay in balance and survive."

Mary paused reflectively, then continued. "We joked about making a cooperative commonwealth, and taking back our government, but we began to act that way in everything that we did. It got to be fun, and we realized that we could have faith in one another and trust one another. That was about the time that we all got into debating the terms of the New Declaration of Independence to say what we were against *and* give our visions of the future. That was a really important stage of our development because we all took part in specifying what we wanted and what therefore *could be* in the future. If you want something real bad, there's always a way that you can get it. I'm convinced of that. People *always* have choices in life, and all it takes is determination to get what you want.

"And don't underestimate the way that initial successes lead to greater and greater momentum for working together and making things happen. Even little things, like defeating a really bad candidate or passing a decent human rights law. And above all, have faith that other people also know what needs to be done and will work together with you when the chips are down. I hope you can have some of that excitement and success in your life, David! And now I've got to go and get dressed."

David could see the pride and emotion in Mary's eyes, and he knew he had glimpsed the passion underlying the years of struggle and achievement of his parents' generation.

"Thanks, Mom," he said quietly. "I think I'll go up to the tower and bug Dad for a while."

I n our usage, *economic nationalism* refers to a package of economic policies that are shaped by or on behalf of (1) the American society as a whole, as an organic community, distinct from all other parts of the world, and (2) the *people* of that community, particularly the great bulk of Americans in the middle of the social pyramid, distinct from corporations, banks, and other interests. Our version of economic nationalism presupposes a democratic decision-making process animated by values such as equality, fairness, and the long-term public interest. Its goals are to serve the needs and wants of Americans in the United States, rather than such abstractions as globalism, free trade, or free markets, which serve chiefly to mask the power and avarice of the transnational corporations, big finance, and wealthy elites.

The Strategy and Principles
of Economic Nationalism

Our basic premise is that the U.S. domestic market is still the strongest and most lucrative in the world. Practically all sellers of goods and services want to sell in the U.S. market for the obvious reason that there is so much purchasing power contained within it. A key element in our strategy is to use the strength of that market as leverage to induce (or force, if necessary) all those who wish to sell in the United States to make a tangible commitment to the economic well-being of Americans. A purposeful U.S. government has many ways to encourage or require the creation of good jobs, new investment, or other economic contribution as a condition of doing business in the United States—and we describe several of them shortly.

A corollary to this central strategic assumption is that U.S. trade policy must be purposeful and selective—from the standpoint of American advantage. That is, there can be no absolutes such as "free trade," but only case-by-case cost-benefit analyses based on the long-term interests of American workers as producers. NAFTA and GATT must be repudiated in those specific cases where their damage to the long-term income prospects of American workers is substantial. In taking this position, we are only being open about policies and practices that our foreign trading "partners" conceal in a variety of ways.

Another cornerstone of our strategy is that issues and issue areas can never be considered singly or in isolation, but only together, as components of a single whole. In isolation, many issues lead to zero-sum games in which short-term thinking, deadlock, high costs, and bitterness are likely products. Together, multiple issues provide opportunities for compromise, cost containment, and solutions that are mutually satisfactory if not complete for any party involved. Moreover, social and economic reality is one integrated whole, and it is this "big picture" over the long term that really matters.

To extend this point a bit, it is also absolutely essential continuously to see politics and economics as interpenetrated and interdependent—not even two sides of the same coin, but a single holograph with different pictures depending on the viewer's perspective. The idea that there is or can be some division between the two is an ideological construct intended to shield economic inequality (produced by the supposedly "neutral, mechanical" workings of the economy) from the visibility that might lead to a "political" choice to moderate it. In reality, the income distribution pattern of the United States is both the product of politics and the producer of politics: where does economics end and politics begin, or politics end and economics begin? Understanding occurs only when the holograph is moved back and forth under the light.

Next, our strategy makes regular use of comparisons with other industrialized democratic countries. In many respects, other such nations are doing better than the United States—providing a higher quality of life at a lower social cost, for example. While their policies are not always transferable to the United States (for a variety of reasons), their experience nevertheless has much to teach us. Are taxes "too high" in the United States? Comparison shows that taxes are much higher in all other industrialized democracies (including Japan, if military spending is removed from the comparison). The issue seems to be who is being taxed and how much (corporations and the wealthy elsewhere, middle-class individuals in the United States), and what people receive in the way of services (more and better elsewhere).

Finally, our strategy sets out the long-term interest of the whole community as the ultimate test of principles and policies. This may require short-term sacrifices on the part of certain interest groups or even entire sectors of the population. We can only do our best to see that such sacrifices are minimized, widely shared, and reasonably justified under all circumstances. Once nearly everybody thinks in terms of the community's long-range needs instead of their own short-term interests, we shall be well on the road to improvement.

We stress four principles of economic nationalism to be implemented using this strategy. The number is arbitrary, of course; we could offer more or fewer. But the point is only to illustrate what the substance of an economic nationalist program would be, and these four principles are enough to make that point.

Create Good Jobs for Americans
in the United States

A "good job" is one that pays a minimum of $12 to $15 an hour, or $25,000 to $30,000 a year in 1992 dollars, plus health care, vacations, and other standard benefits. And the working conditions must be safe, humane, and reasonably satisfying to the workers involved.

Jobs of this kind have been lost in recent years because of the relocation of manufacturing to low-wage areas of the world and the advent of new technologies that permit increased production with fewer employees. Not surprisingly, corporate profits have risen sharply at the same time that U.S. wage levels have stagnated or dropped in real terms.

What can be done to change this supposedly unavoidable result of that supposedly impersonal machine known as the free market? The general answer is simple: assert some political (i.e., democratically generated) controls over corporate profit maximization so that the economic rights of workers get included as one of the necessary costs of doing business. Workers in several European countries have higher wages, longer vacations, and better pensions than American workers. Why?

Of course there will be a howl of outrage from the financial elite and the corporations. The principle of people before profits *does* mean that new values must take precedence, and a different set of priorities for doing business must then follow. (This principle must be fought for, and established, through a revived democratic political process, as we describe in the next chapters.) Once the principle is established, many more specific answers can then follow.

To start, we could practice damage control in any one of several forms. A Corporate Responsibility Program could require not only advance notice of intended closure or relocation of major facilities but also substantial closure/departure payments, some directly to workers and some into a combined retraining/pension fund set up by the U.S. government.

Or a system of capital controls could be instituted so that capital flight to other countries would be inhibited and/or penalized by taxes unless an equivalent number of good jobs were created in the United States by the same corporation. If preservation of good jobs in the United States were given primary consideration, tax credits or even subsidies could be orchestrated so as to enable potential runaway businesses to remain in the United States. It would be less disruptive to hold on to what we have now than to have to create new opportunities.

Next, the policy trend of constantly shrinking corporate income taxes should be reversed. A significant new level of income taxation should be instituted, but with substantial deductions for producing new good jobs in the United States. At the same time, comparable requirements should be built into import duties on goods and services produced elsewhere for sale in the United States. The revenue impact must be exactly the same for corporations with headquarters in the United States as for those based in other countries: all must feel an equivalent pressure to create new good jobs in the United States. Exactly what such jobs should be is best left to the corporations themselves; all that need be required is a quality level that meets our definition.

A portion of the new revenues derived from taxes and import duties should be allocated to public corporations responsible for training workers and sustaining them in on-the-job learning situations. With a continuing emphasis on developing the American workforce's flexibility and capability, there will be fewer reasons for capital flight in the first place.

Another portion of those new revenues should be devoted to providing opportunities for people to develop their skills and get financial support for starting their own businesses. A systematic program of encouragement for new small-business creation will both provide an outlet for innovative ideas and energy and serve as a supplement to worker retraining programs.

Finally, a commitment to good jobs for Americans must include creation of public-service jobs financed by the national government. Many tasks need to be done to catch up with past failures to maintain and repair existing infrastructure or to train and develop our working population. Public-service jobs could be a very large component of the essential work to be done —and not just a residual category. Programs for national service by young people should be expanded to generate low-cost supplementary support for many state and local functions. The point is to expand the infrastructure and local support that enables business to prosper and jobs to be created.

Close the Outrageous Income Gap

The newly global and financialized version of capitalism that has been taking shape for the past several years systematically generates vast wealth at the very top—for no more than 5 percent of U.S. families—while everybody else remains at their existing level or actually loses shares of national income. This trend has been spurred for the past two decades by a continuing series of tax cuts for the very rich, creating the greatest disparity between rich and poor ever known in American history. The resulting income distribution pattern is economically unproductive and inefficient, morally and socially unjustifiable, and politically dangerous.

A program for closing this gap should include raising the incomes of the middle and lower levels; assuring them against falling back again because of sickness, aging, accident, divorce, and so on; providing new opportunities for many of them to rise to higher levels; and restoring the principle that the rich can afford to pay taxes. (Again, a revived democratic political process will be required to accomplish these goals.)

A vigorous job-creation program will first put the middle class back to work and restore benefits and pension rights. Roughly 30 million families have suffered some form of actual job, benefit, or income loss in the past twenty years. Because these workers have skills, experience, and a willing work ethic, they should be absorbed in upgraded jobs quite readily.

Developing skills and fostering employment for the nearly 30 million U.S. families earning from zero to $20,000 will be a much greater challenge. Reduced periods of welfare eligibility (except for the truly incapable) will be of some help, but the primary task is to enable this sector of the population to find the skills, self-confidence, and motivation to go to work—*and to have appropriate jobs available for them.*

All levels of the private sector must be encouraged, induced, and if necessary subsidized to provide work opportunities that pay at least the minimum wage, which in turn must be steadily increased toward a five-year goal in the $8 to $10 per hour range. Public support for enterprise zones close to low-income populations, or for moving people to job sites, makes economic sense. So does public support for extended periods of paid internships or public-service work, during which people can learn skills and self-reliance. Low-income and dependent sectors of the population must be reintegrated into the society, lest they be left behind in a semipermanent underclass, and work opportunities are the key to doing this.

No program for closing today's vast and growing income gap can be complete, however, without a major new commitment to the principle of progressive income taxation: that those who make more money should pay a larger share of their income in taxes. The concept of progressive taxation reflects the value judgment that those who are specially favored by the structure and workings of our economy should contribute relatively more to accomplishing society's shared social purposes. A progressive income tax, including a substantial corporate income tax, also provides a means of deploying incentives in the form of deductions to private firms and individuals for acting in socially desirable ways, such as by creating new jobs or making desired investments.

As figure 1.1 demonstrated, progressive corporate income taxes used to make up a substantial share of federal revenues, and the capital gains, inheritance, and estate taxes were real factors in producing revenue. Tax rates in the 1950s ran up to 90 percent on earnings over certain amounts. In the 1990s, the corporate income tax produces a negligible share of federal revenues, capital gains have been cut way back, inheritance and estate taxes have been practically eliminated, and the maximum tax on earnings is 39.6 percent.

Moreover, almost every recent change has been in the direction of making taxes more regressive—that is, making them a heavier burden for poorer people than for the wealthy. Tax "simplification" is certainly desirable, but most of what is offered as simplification is instead a thinly veiled attempt to reduce further what progressivity remains in the federal system. The idea of a flat tax, in which all people pay the same share of their income in taxes, is a good example. It sounds simple and perhaps fair, but 15 percent or 20 percent of a $25,000 income is a much heavier hit for a family to take than it would be for a family earning $250,000 a year.

There should also be a limit on what people are entitled to receive without engaging in any productive activity at all—that is, from dividends, interest, rent, or financial speculation. And there should be a maximum level of compensation for corporate executives, beyond which taxes rise sharply. The United States is rapidly developing an elite group in this category, and American corporate executives make many times larger salaries than their counterparts in the other industrialized countries.

There is thus a very strong case for reasserting progressive taxation, and it does not require any new or untested departures in public policy. Merely by restoring the tax law provisions of the 1940s and 1950s—the years of our greatest economic expansion and success—the U.S. government could realize additional revenues of about $150 billion per year. In other words, we could finance the entire job-creation and public investment program *and* close the income gap with one "back to the future" policy choice!

An Aggressive Trade Policy

Trade policy, a high-stakes game, has two primary goals: seeing that goods and services made in the United States can gain access to and be competitive in foreign countries, and conditioning access to the U.S. market so that good jobs in the United States are maximized and imports are roughly in balance with exports. Import duties are an integral part of an aggressive trade policy. Tradeoffs are likely, and retaliation is always a possibility; judgments about comparative advantages are continually necessary.

The crucial first principle for American negotiators is that the United States is the world's most lucrative single market, and every producer wants very much to sell here. The second is that such ideological absolutes as free trade and laissez-faire must give way to practical case-by-case calculations of costs and benefits in terms of jobs for Americans in the United States.

To promote full (not token) access to foreign markets on behalf of goods and services made by Americans, U.S. government policy ultimately has to be ready to deny access to the U.S. market to some countries or products made in them. Vague promises, for which the Japanese (among others) are famous, cannot be accepted. Actual practice is the test of whether goods and services made in the United States do or do not have full access to foreign markets. It may also be necessary to provide public subsidies in order for U.S.-made products to compete with products subsidized by foreign governments. The United States should be ready and able to do so, as part of a program to protect and expand U.S. jobs. We can be far tougher than we have been about demanding access to foreign markets.

The principle of conditioning access to our own market not only makes conflict with other countries more likely, but might add to the difficulty of gaining access to foreign markets. Can we or should we impose limits and requirements on foreign countries and producers at the same time as we demand unlimited access to their markets? The answer is a resounding *yes,* because that is precisely what the game of international trade is about. There are no points in this game for consistency, but only for the number of good jobs for Americans in the United States.

Of course there will be conflict, and hard bargaining, and eventual compromises in which we shall not get everything we would like to have. But we can get far more than we have to date by being much tougher and readier to impose real sanctions, accepting only practice and not promises, and being ready to suffer some retaliation if necessary. We can cushion the effects of retaliation if desired, but we cannot bend to the complaints of frightened U.S. exporters on every occasion when they feel threatened. Our common interest, as measured particularly by good jobs, must take precedence.

The larger goal to be served by all these policies is to assure that the dollar value of imports does not greatly exceed the dollar value of exports in any given year. The purpose of balancing imports against exports is to avoid a seriously negative balance of payments (more dollars paid out for the purchase of imports than brought back from the sale of exports) that weakens the value of the dollar among global currencies. No single factor (not even chronic annual federal government deficits) so quickly undermines the dollar's value compared to other world currencies as a net trade deficit, which has been running over $100 billion in each of the past several years.

How can these goals be accomplished? There are many ways, if only we want to employ them. "Domestic content" requirements can simply require that goods sold in the United States have a certain proportion of components made in the United States, or that they be assembled in the United States, or that services be provided only through employment of a certain proportion of Americans, and so on. Substantial duties can be imposed on selected or all imports, with equally substantial deductions for creation of identified jobs, or for particular kinds of investments in the United States, or for whatever specific behavior we deem to be in our public interest. Less drastic policies include "voluntary" quotas or contributions of various kinds that accomplish the same results.

All these policies, of course, are flagrant violations of the NAFTA and GATT treaties. But those treaties were never intended to advantage American workers or American small businesses. They were intended only for the profit maximization of the transnational corporations, banks, and global financial elite, organized under the banner of globalism and free trade. Some specific repudiation of their provisions on a case-by-case basis is essential, and we should be open about it. To a considerable extent, our trading "partners" do this all the time, only much less openly.

An economic nationalist trade policy carries implications for a new posture in foreign affairs generally and the role of the military specifically. The U.S. government should not seek to create a world in our image or to serve as the world's policeman. World hegemony is no longer possible economically or in terms of the time and energy diverted from our own domestic problems. The dollar does not have to be the world's common-denominator currency, although that has been beneficial to the United States in the past and should continue to be under most circumstances. We should not try to solve centuries-old ethnic or religious conflicts around the world or accept responsibility to cure problems not of our creation.

The United States should seek to maintain equitable trading arrangements, necessary access to resources, and fulfillment of obligations, in a world dominated by no "superpower" but only by the stronger economies—a Germany-led Europe, Japan, China, and perhaps India or even Russia. This is a balance-of-power situation, in which our interest will always be to side with the weaker nation or bloc of nations to preserve rough parity among all major economic units of the world.

Military policy should be designed to serve this basic foreign policy. The giant budget appropriations of the Cold War years are no longer necessary. Research and development should go forward, but procurement can be held to the minimum necessary to maintain a technological edge for relatively small rapid-deployment forces. But arms sales must be contained, on the part of United States and foreign manufacturers alike, both in order to reduce the prospects of small wars and to preserve the American edge in weapons capabilities.

The United States will not need bases all over the world. We will have to learn to accept the fact that people will do bad things to one another without feeling that we have to do more than set a better example. We should have alternative supplies available and conservation policies in place so that we are never again subject to blackmail by oil companies and Middle Eastern governments. Instead, priority should be given to sophisticated protection against terrorism in the United States and (perhaps) greatly reduced access across U.S. borders.

This brings us to the very sensitive subject of immigration policy. A rational economic nationalist program does not require a complete shutdown of immigration. The United States has always been the land of immigrants and a beacon of opportunity for aspiring people of the world, and it has gained immeasurably from their hard work. Our own self-image is bound up with remaining the land of opportunity, and it would be much better for us to develop the jobs that enable us to accommodate a reasonable number of immigrants.

But there is nothing wrong with putting effective limits on the numbers of various people invited to enter the United States in the future. We could select by occupational capabilities, or for political or family reasons, or for combinations of them. The American community can decide what outsiders it is willing to invite to join it; it does not have to accept the self-nominations of millions of individuals from all over the world. There are, after all, limits to the population-sustaining capability of this sector of the planet. And when immigrants are invited to join, there is every reason to require that they learn English and assimilate to the common-denominator features of American life—whatever the cultural islands in which they may choose to live.

A Fiscal Policy in the Long-Term National Interest

The basic problem of U.S. fiscal policy was succinctly stated in chapter 2: regular spending in excess of revenues so that annual deficits in the hundreds of billions of dollars have cumulated into a huge national debt that threatens either collapse or paralysis by about 2020. Interest on this debt, compounding implacably every day, will soon become the largest single item of federal spending.

Blame for this situation is often placed on the individual "entitlements" built into federal statutes, whereby people who fulfill certain conditions are entitled to prescribed benefits or services. As figure 2.2 (p. 42) showed, "no change" assumptions result in entitlement spending in excess of revenues early in the twenty-first century.

There are many entitlement programs with different beneficiaries, including some that grant tax credits, deductions, or other loopholes to corporations and wealthy individuals. Most, however, form important parts of the social safety net, protecting against a variety of misfortunes that can occur to people. The largest entitlements are Social Security, Medicare, and Medicaid. The first two of these are supposedly sustained by trust funds whose revenues come from payroll taxes.

Two forces are driving the trust funds, and the federal government, into apparent fiscal crisis. The first is the demography of the country: our population is getting older, and living longer, and the huge "baby boom" generation will reach retirement age early in the twenty-first century. Within a roughly ten-year span in that period, the ratio of workers paying into the systems to recipients of benefits will drop from five-to-one to three-to-one.

The second is the relentlessly rising cost of health care, at a rate more than double that of inflation and adding tens of billions of dollars to federal spending every year. More people are living longer, and terminal illnesses are hugely expensive; combined with rapidly rising health-care costs overall, this makes for a situation often described as an "entitlement crisis."

But such a definition should be rejected. There are two sides to fiscal policy: *revenues* and *expenditures*. "Entitlements" are expenditures that Congress has chosen to set up as automatic payments to people who fit certain conditions. Revenues are the sum total of similar choices made by Congress about who should pay taxes, at what levels, and with what exemptions, credits, and deductions. Fiscal policy must be evaluated holistically, in terms of *both* sources and levels of revenues *and* objects of expenditures, including entitlement expenditures. Such an analysis suggests at the least that our fiscal crisis is not *merely* a problem of entitlements: it is also a problem of *who* pays taxes, and *how much*—and with what opportunities to reduce taxes owed or avoid them entirely.

Looked at this way, any solution should consider *both* tax changes and entitlement limits. And there *must* be a solution—a new fiscal policy that balances the national government budget by at least 2004. Payments of interest on the debt, essentially a transfer from ordinary citizen-taxpayers to the wealthy who hold that debt, must be reduced to manageable levels. The U.S. government cannot remain dependent on foreign capital to finance its annual deficits and/or the refinancing of the debt. A balanced budget is also essential to hold down interest rates, revive our savings and investment rates, make capital available for private investment, and restore flexibility and choice over current public investment in infrastructure or human development.

The budget need not be in precise balance every year. There must be some capacity to incur a deficit to stimulate the economy in a time of recession or in other emergencies. But it must be in balance over the course of the business cycle; for every deficit, there must be a compensating surplus. This can be accomplished by an exercise of political will and determination, from a perspective that puts the long-term public interest first, accompanied by the principles of shared sacrifice and overall fairness.

Amending the Constitution to achieve this goal is unnecessary, essentially an illusion that avoids the real choices involved. Only political will and determination can do the job, and this depends on the people rising above immediate self-interest. The people will have to force their "leaders" to stop posturing and competing with one another to offer tax cuts—tax cuts that always disproportionately favor the wealthy and continue to shift the tax burden to the middle class.

In this regard, the lessons of 1993–95 must be learned. There was a modest and successful effort to reduce the deficit-debt spiral in 1993, which resulted in some short-term improvement. It was followed, after the election of 1994, by renewed efforts to cut taxes and add greatly to future deficits. Were the people to blame, or their leaders? We think the latter, and propose a balanced-budget program here—with ways that the people can enforce it in the next chapter.

This is a middle-class balanced-budget program that addresses both revenues and entitlements and is based on four premises. First, the middle class should bear no larger tax burden; if others pay their fair share in a progressive tax system, that burden could even be reduced. Second, reform of Social Security and Medicare should involve shared sacrifice progressively implemented and generational equity. Younger people must not be asked to make much higher contributions because there are so many older people drawing benefits, and they must be able to count on receiving benefits when they retire. Third, changes in Social Security and other entitlements must be made gradually so that people can plan well in advance. Fourth, all proposals must be based on a long-term perspective of at least forty years, as well as a holistic and public-interest orientation. We propose a ten-point program.

1. *Plug tax loopholes.* Eliminate U.S. tax credits for taxes that corporations pay to foreign countries. Tax profits made overseas annually, without waiting until they are "repatriated" to the United States. Prevent both U.S. and foreign multinationals from juggling their books to avoid U.S. taxes. Limit home-mortgage interest deductions to mortgage loans of $200,000 or less. Tax capital gains at the same rate as ordinary income.

2. *Restore progressivity to the tax system.* Abandon all "flat tax" and "consumption tax" ideas, and instead simplify by eliminating most deductions, substantially increasing personal exemptions, and raising the marginal rate on incomes over $250,000 to 67 percent. Restore the corporate income tax to levels comparable to other industrial countries, that is, about 35

percent on net profits over a fixed amount per year. Restore the estate, inheritance, and gift taxes to their economy-building 1950 levels.

3. Enact an "affluence test" for all federal benefits, including Social Security, and restore a viable social safety net. For all those with incomes more than 300 percent over the median national income, begin reducing benefits in steps of 10 percent for each $10,000 of income, but cap the reduction at 80 percent so that all receive something for their contributions. This means that reductions would start at an income of about $100,000 per year in 1994 dollars.

A reconstructed social safety net must be available to enable people to hold on to their gains and feel a sense of security about the future. Some contributions from employers and individuals should be expected, but the system should be backed by general revenues. Work should be rewarded, principally because it is the defining feature of the middle class. Those who earn income, whether as employees or as self-employed, should be entitled to a higher level and/or longer term of entitlement to benefits, based on the number of quarters in the immediate past five years that they actually worked.

Some form of cost-controlled national health-care system, probably the Canadian model, must be instituted. Individual choices can be maximized and portability assured, as well as costs more effectively controlled, within such a single-payer system. A separate public corporation supported by general revenues would make sense.

A reconstructed Social Security system should be integrated with unemployment and disability funding to provide modest and needs-tested but comprehensive economic security for all. The only long-term means of reforming the welfare system is to multiply available jobs, child-care and educational opportunities, and mental/physical assistance programs; the real problem is the proportion of hard-core welfare recipients who are the products of dysfunctional families. Time limits and work requirements are a modest start, not a cure. But there must be a means of providing assistance for the truly needy. The cost is not prohibitive in the context of other budget changes proposed.

4. Change Social Security and Medicare contributions to make them less regressive. Employers and employees now contribute 7.65 percent of the employee's income to Social Security and 1.5 percent to Medicare, up to a maximum of $62,500 of income per year in the case of Social Security. Reduce employee contribution rates on incomes less than $20,000 to 5 percent. Raise employee contribution rates on incomes of more than $100,000 to 10 percent. Make all income subject to Social Security and Medicare contributions. Reduce rates on self-employed people from the present 15.3 percent to 10 percent.

5. Limit the rise in Social Security retirement age, and offer incentives instead. The retirement age is being lifted to sixty-seven in steps to be completed by 2022. While this could be rescheduled to 2010 to realize some baby-boom savings, it must be the last such increase. Higher benefits could be paid if benefits are not drawn until age seventy; or widow(er) benefits could be expanded in exchange for such deferral. But the early retirement age should be held at sixty-two to open up more jobs for younger people.

6. Reform Medicare, Medicaid, and the tax system to cap and control health-care costs. The entitlement side of the fiscal problem cannot be managed unless ballooning health-care costs are addressed. Plan to phase Medicare and Medicaid eventually into a national single-payer system where cost controls can be imposed. Until then, require Medicare/Medicaid providers to justify in detail any increases above inflation.

7. Restrict congressional and other federal pension programs and refine inflation measures. Limit the huge pensions that Congress has provided for itself by converting them to annuities equivalent to that of the average private-sector worker. Limit federal employees' and armed forces pensions and increase the number of years of service required for retirement (and/or delay payment until retirement age). Refine the consumer price index (CPI) or other inflation measures to ensure that cost-of-living adjustments (COLAs) are accurate reflections of purchasing power changes. Set COLAs for all federal benefit programs to lag behind inflation by 1 percent per year.

8. *Reorganize the national government's budget system.* The U.S. government's budget is chaotic and deliberately misleading. First, devise one operating budget in which all costs of running the government's day-to-day activities are clearly set forth, and another capital budget in which long-term capital investments such as transportation facilities, land, buildings, and so forth are separately detailed. All the states and every major business have two such budgets so that these very different kinds of expenditures can be seen (and perhaps funded) separately.

Second, consolidate the hundreds of "off-budget" entities, trust funds, guarantees, and other hidden programs into this set of two budgets so that it is possible to grasp clearly what the government is doing and what its direct and contingent obligations are. Finally, develop some way of budgeting over a longer time frame, perhaps three or four years for the operating budget and ten years for the capital budget. Annual refinements can still be made, but at least some planning would be possible and the time saved by avoiding the every-year budget battle applied to other tasks.

9. *Shift discretionary expenditures away from defense and toward domestic public investment.* This program will reduce entitlement spending, raise revenues, and reduce payment of interest on the national debt. In other words, it will free up substantial funds for discretionary use. But defense will not require the level of spending of the immediate past. The government will finally be able to address the public investment needs that have been deferred for so long: transportation and communications

infrastructure, education, research and development, and technological innovation. Not least, this will lead to development of millions of new public- and private-sector jobs for Americans in the United States.

Private investment must also be vigorously promoted. Today, it is shaped by short-term thinking and maximum profit opportunities, which too often has meant speculation in currency or other financial markets and/or new capital facilities in Third World countries. This mind-set will have to be altered to bring about adequate levels of investment in new productive facilities in the United States.

One means of doing this is through tax policy. If substantial income taxes are in place, offer deductions or credits for job-producing investments in the United States, or impose punitive taxes on capital gains from investments in speculative transactions or other countries. Greatly increased investment in the United States is too important to be left to chance.

Another means is outright capital controls, by which capital can be prevented from being invested outside the United States. Although this is usually considered a drastic step requiring vast oversight and an army of electronic accountants, more moderate versions could be implemented. Even the credible threat, moreover, might be sufficient to gain the cooperation of most transnational corporations and banks.

10. *Impose additional taxes on gasoline, with the proceeds transferred to the states.* There are several purposes in adding perhaps 50 cents to the existing federal gas tax: to reduce air pollution, reduce our high and growing dependence on imported oil, conserve oil resources, and find a source for providing revenues to the states. The latter often are unable to raise adequate revenues within their own borders because of interstate competition. Exemptions could be made or refunds provided for genuine hardship cases, for example, low-income people without access to public transportation who have daily commutes over a certain mileage.

Summary: What Have We Done?

We have deliberately been detailed and specific in this chapter in order to show that there *are* readily available means of solving our economic problems. These principles of economic nationalism will make for a dramatic change in the American economy and particularly in its distribution of income among Americans. Middle-class jobs and security will be assured in the context of a balanced budget, which in turn will help keep interest rates down and stabilize the value of the dollar. The new trade policy will antagonize some other countries but on balance will provide net gains for American jobs and basic prosperity.

Essential fairness will pervade the entire economic system, from progressive taxation to the social safety net to the reconstruction of Social Security. Vigorous promotion of the opportunities of the middle will also pull the underclass back into the social order and reassure the upper levels that the country will be economically productive and socially and politically stable in the future.

All of this assumes, of course, that the components of the economic nationalist program can actually be implemented through the U.S. political system. It will take some fundamental reconstruction of that system before it can finally be accomplished. But it *is* possible, and we now turn to ways of doing it.

FIVE

"Each Generation Has the Right to Choose for Itself"

David knocked gently in greeting as he entered the tower, pleased to find his father waiting for him. Dad must be getting into this too, he thought; usually he would be locked up in intense electronic communications or fiercely concentrating on a repair job with parts spread out all over the table and floor.

"Ah, the historian! What took you so long to report for work today?" Jeff asked with a welcoming smile, and gestured at the only other chair in the room.

"Well, Mom got a bit wound up, I guess," David answered cheerfully. "Maybe it was all the good questions I asked."

"More likely she wanted to tell you all about the importance of having an economic program, and that you can't fight something with nothing," Jeff countered.

"Well, yes." David realized he was learning things about his parents and their relationship as well as about their political experiences. "But she also referred to your sense of intangible, sort of spiritual, forces that move people to trust one another and act in unison at particular times."

Jeff looked at his son with new appreciation, and spoke thoughtfully. "Okay, you're coming on as an interviewer, David. Your mom and I used to argue interminably about the relative importance of program, vision, and process—until we finally agreed that all three are equally important, though maybe in a different mix at different times. I was always the vision and process person, of course, and your bright and linear mother was always on the program side."

"Your turn, Dad." David pressed his opportunity. "Talk about vision and process."

Jeff first leaned back in his chair and put his feet up in a move that reminded David of his mother about half an hour ago. "People have to have general goals as well as specific ones, David, and a morally justifiable, uplifting purpose for acting together. Anger and frustration can get you started, but they don't keep you going very long.

"We all need a vision of a future that is worth sacrificing for, even dying for if we have to, that is justified by something much higher than anybody's self-interest today. You can't envision such a future just by projecting from the present, or by emphasizing material things. You have to have faith in people and in a possible future that can't be fully described from the present but is terribly important for your children and grandchildren. You need something like a spiritual reawakening, almost a rebirth of a sense of community, a mutual trust and confidence that people can really work together and do things that are in their shared common interest over the long term. Something has to rally you into action!"

David was silent for a moment, processing his father's obviously powerful feelings. "Mom mentioned that there was a time when it seemed like everybody was rewriting the Declaration of Independence," he finally probed.

"I thought you'd never ask." Jeff grinned, holding up a frayed document with two fingers. "Here's the hard copy that we all voted on, on the Fourth of July, 2000. The debate before that was really something! Proposals and counterproposals were flashing across thousands of screens all across the country. There must have been at least 10,000 originally proposed by individuals and groups when the call first went out as the year 2000 approached. Then they had to be fed through a long process of finding common themes, agreeing on the basic points, and so forth. I must have seen and commented on fifty drafts myself. But finally several of the independent parties all agreed on a single version at their conventions in 2000. And of course it gave the movement a focus and sense of purpose that it had never had!"

David by this time knew the document very well. "How and why did the movement write 10,000 of these in a year or so?" he asked incredulously.

Jeff was pleased to see David's appreciation, but eager to make his point. "We knew we had to educate ourselves, and break out of the frustrating, resentful passivity of the 1990s somehow. It's absolutely crucial that people come to envision what they want, and what could be theirs, if they are willing to work together for it. But they have to do this by themselves, individually, and it can never be done for them by somebody else. That's why we all had to write our own Declarations of Independence, to recapture the boldness and determination and vision of 1776, and really come to think of ourselves as able to do something similar about our own situation.

"We studied not only 1776, but Jefferson and Jackson and 1848 and Seneca Falls, Abraham Lincoln in the 1860s, 1896 and all the Populist Party declarations and platforms, Teddy Roosevelt's New Nationalism and Franklin Roosevelt's New Deal. But we finally decided that we needed something rooted in our past but fundamentally new and addressed to the future, not warmed-over anything. How would it have struck you in 2000?"

"Well, Dad," David said slowly, still struggling with the enormity of the debate a dozen years earlier. He finally ventured, "There's a lot of God stuff in here, more than I would have expected."

Jeff looked up at him seriously. "Yes, I suppose so. But when you set out on a totally unprecedented course, in the kind of economic crisis we were in, you have to reach back for some source of faith and hope. We had to trust in God and one another in the vulnerable way that people feel when they are alone in a really threatening situation—remember the old saying that there are no atheists in foxholes? We were more genuinely spiritual than I ever was or expected to be at any time before. David, it was a time of reawakening and incredible inspiration!"

Jeff paused in some old-fashioned embarrassment at showing such emotion in front of his son, but then took David's hand and completed his thought. "Of course we fell short, but not for lack of trying. And we're still working on it, although because we've done so much, the urgency is kind of less today."

David could *feel* the excitement of the times his father had been part of, and wanted badly to share more fully in it. But he held to his role and purpose. "How long before you brought out the constitutional amendments, Dad? Was it the same kind of debate over them?"

"Oh, the amendments were in draft discussion form before the Declaration was approved," Jeff confided. "They were the specific visions that implemented the big one, so they had to wait for it to pave the way. And, yes, there was a similar debate, and it really helped people to see their goals more concretely. Then they were ready for the years of organizing and campaigning to get them approved!"

"What about process, Dad? Why do you always link vision with process, and both with program?"

Jeff sighed. "How you do something is fundamentally linked to what you want to achieve. You have to act today in terms of the values that you want to have paramount in the future you seek. You can't violate principles you believe in, unless that's the only way you can survive. Nobody can build a peaceful, decent society through violence, unless it's forced upon them in self-defense.

"Second, you have to think in terms of how things *could be*, rather than how they are. There's a constant need to remind one another of what we want, and how to act today in terms of tomorrow. And you have to fit your process of change to what people can realistically *do* in their real lives, even assuming that they care profoundly for the goals you all share.

"That's why we had such emphasis on communications through electronic mail, faxes, and the internet, supplemented by old-fashioned postal mail. We had to avoid the kind of burnout that 1960s people experienced with two or three years of constant meetings and all that local neighborhood organizing emphasis. Of course, that wasn't all of the 1960s stuff we wanted to avoid.

"It was important, particularly for people who kept thinking of the sixties as a time of failure, to make clear that this time was really different: we had the great bulk of the middle class with us, and lots of blue-collar workers. College kids were pretty much out of it, and that was good.

"For example, we wanted to minimize the number of times that people had to come out for meetings and planning sessions, so they could have a life and remain energetic for our cause. We brought folks together for face-to-face rallies and demonstrations from time to time, primarily so that they could *see* one another—how many they were, and all together—and to impress the media, which helped us gain visibility."

Jeff relaxed and added with pride, "And, of course, we had to give content to our vision and focus to our organizing efforts—which meant that we had to have a *program* that reflected and implemented all we stood for and sought. And so we had to turn to people like your mother, who had been arguing that all along."

"Sounds like you're saying that you needed one another, all right," David summed up, "and maybe that you still do," he added gratuitously.

Jeff smiled blandly, and parried. "Wouldn't that be another assignment, in another course?"

David grinned and closed his notebook.

Visions of achievable futures are crucial to political reconstruction because they mobilize people into action, crystallize social purpose, and provide moral justification for struggle and sacrifice. Such visions may take varying forms, or play different roles, at different times. The vision provided by the New Declaration of Independence, for example, is a comprehensive one linking people to a noble heritage, identifying what is wrong today, and setting forth multiple but very general goals for a sustained movement. It is a stirring vision of a desirable future, and a strong summary statement about the Jeffersonian character of the revolution.

Visions must also take more specific and concrete form, addressed to righting particular wrongs, within the framework provided by the general call to arms of the Declaration. They must be detailed enough to be credible and thus contribute to implementing the larger vision. There are two sets of such visions here, addressed to two key areas of our politics and governance, both of which are entirely consistent with Jefferson's major principles.

First is a vision of a new relationship between citizens and the institutions, officeholders, and policies of their government —essentially the electoral and policymaking processes and their linkage. The system that no longer works is a representative one, in which candidates of two major parties compete in winner-take-all elections for the opportunity to make public policy on behalf of all the citizens. Campaign contributors have enormous leverage over who can be candidates, whether they will be elected, and how they will act once in office.

We envision a system in which all major decisions will be made by the citizenry, after appropriate dialogue and reflection. Members of Congress, elected by proportional voting, will have as their primary functions the framing of issues for popular decision making and the implementation of those decisions. Campaign contributors' political leverage will be sharply limited as part of building a politics of issues and independents. Three constitutional amendments to implement these goals are presented shortly under the heading "Elections and Policymaking."

Second is a vision of the process of governing as it is divided between the central government and the states. The purpose of such change is to reallocate functions and funding sources among them, and to modify the way they perform certain key functions. The system that no longer works is top-heavy at the center, with too much control in the hands of lobbyists and special interests in Washington, D.C., and too many powers centralized in an isolated and out-of-touch bureaucracy. In particular, it has magnified the roles of courts and lawyers, and the rights of criminals, beyond the range of reason.

We envision reducing and decentralizing central government functions so that the different needs of different regions can be flexibly served. Some functions must be devolved to the states, along with revenues required to perform them. Although lobbyists and special interests are active at the state level as well, their resources and energies will at least be dispersed and diluted by having fifty centers of policymaking instead of just one. We also propose restrictions on litigation and lawyers at both federal and state levels. A constitutional amendment and new federal statutes to accomplish these goals will be presented shortly under the heading "Governance Functions."

To be credible and achievable, and yet capable of bringing about the scope and character of change that our circumstances require, these visions must be cast in the form of amendments to the Constitution. We digress briefly to provide some background about this choice and then return to describe our goals and the nature of the amendments to implement them.

Making Visions Practical and Realizable

The cumulative effect of the major proposals we are about to make will add up to substantial change in our governance system, more than at any time since the Constitution was originally drafted and ratified. We argued earlier that constitutional change is overdue and entirely appropriate, particularly since these changes are the minimum necessary for coping with the situation the United States faces today while preserving our democracy. We argue now that they can also fit comfortably within the existing constitutional framework and can be accomplished through an entirely practical and relatively brief set of constitutional amendments.

A constitutional amendment is required in order to change the express terms (and interpretations) of the Constitution, or to change the laws and practices of all the states in a single moment. There is a procedure for the states to petition Congress to call a constitutional convention for the purpose of drafting amendments, but it has never been used. The usual procedure, by which twenty-seven amendments have been added to the Constitution, is for Congress to propose a specific amendment by a two-thirds vote in each house and send it to the states. The amendment is declared part of the Constitution when three-quarters of the state legislatures have passed it by majority vote of both houses.

Some amendments are quite lengthy, particularly those dealing with elections, terms of office, and succession in the case of the presidency. Most, however, are short and simple declarations of rights, powers, or prohibitions. The usual period from congressional approval to state ratification is two or three years, but fast action is possible when circumstances seem compelling. The Twenty-sixth Amendment, for example, which granted the right to vote to eighteen-year-olds in both state and federal elections, was ratified in just over three months in the spring of 1971.

Amending the Constitution is not something that Americans take lightly, and there are several grounds on which opposition is likely. One is that many people view the Constitution as such a stunning achievement that the Founders' work cannot be improved on, and therefore no attempts should be made to do so. Others simply do not welcome change of any kind; at the least, it seems likely to add even more uncertainty to an already threatening world, and there is no guarantee that change will result in improvement. Constitutional scholars, apprehensive lest their expertise be outdated, always warn of unintended consequences and dangers in any proposed change. And then there are people and groups who fundamentally disagree with the values and policy direction represented by the proposed amendment.

In considering the difficulty of accomplishing several amendments in a relatively short period of time, it may be helpful to recall the difficulties faced by the Founding Fathers in getting the necessary nine states to ratify the original Constitution. The original version was highly controversial and bitterly resisted, and it eventually won adoption only by the smallest margin and after several compromises. Its adoption in less than a year was the supreme success of a well-organized group that employed multiple means of persuasion and unrelenting pressure in the several states.

A similar campaign will undoubtedly be needed in our immediate future, beginning with the task of getting two-thirds votes in each house of Congress as it is constituted today. This will undoubtedly involve a major national debate and efforts at the grassroots in every state, and probably will require the concentrated efforts of new independent parties and more than one election to develop the necessary support. Then the campaign must move to the ratification process in the states, again grounded in local districts. Despite the obvious difficulties, the Founders' success offers both a model and hope.

We believe that while some changes can be accomplished by federal statute, it would be preferable to accomplish all major changes through constitutional amendments. In this way, a clear and legitimate mandate would be achieved, national uniformity would be assured, and the changes could all be implemented at the same time. Although this would risk offending the sensitivities of some of the states, it is fully precedented (as in the Twenty-sixth Amendment noted earlier) and far more efficient. Four amendments of reasonable length and limited complexity are all that are required.

Elections and Policymaking

Our goal is an issue-based direct democracy grounded in independent thinking unaffected by the two moribund major parties or the money of campaign contributors. We believe this is the only means of restoring popular control over, and therefore confidence in, the national government. To achieve this goal, five principles must be established in law and practice.

1. *Major issues must be decided by the people.* In this section, we are adapting well-established procedures for initiatives and referendums from several states to the national level. "Major issues" would include significant change in entitlement programs, tax policy, spending levels and priorities, trade policy, immigration, governance mechanisms for the money system or the environment, and the like. In specific cases, what is a "major" issue or a big enough policy change to require popular vote will initially be decided by Congress. But 5 percent of those voting in the last presidential election (about 6 or 7 million people by 2000) could by electronic petition bring about a popular vote on any issue that Congress failed to send out to the people.

This procedure would effectively reduce the discretionary roles of Congress and the president in the policymaking process. The primary tasks of Congress would be to frame issues for decision by the people and to carry out those decisions when made. The president's veto power would not apply to decisions made by the voters; however, the president would retain his current powers to act in emergencies, foreign or domestic. Congress's current powers to confirm or reject such actions (e.g., the sending of troops to potential combat) would devolve to the people in major cases.

Officeholders in Congress would serve in the relatively confined role of delegates, rather than free-agent "representatives." Nevertheless, they would still have power to make minor and implementing laws, which would be subject to presidential veto. All such actions by Congress would be subject to referendum when challenged by electronic petition from people making up 5 percent of those voting in the last presidential election. Similarly, the same 5 percent total could propose an initiative to Congress, which, if not enacted by Congress, would be passed to the voters at the next general election.

Initiatives, referendums, and popular votes on major issues

would be scheduled on a quarterly basis so that delays in acting would be minimized. A sixty-day debate and discussion period would be required before any matter could be voted on. As in most states, the relatively nonpartisan attorney general would provide the ballot descriptions of the changes proposed and describe their probable effects, in electronically available forms, at the start of this sixty-day period. Members of Congress would be empowered to add brief arguments for and against each proposal. This quarterly vote would be subject to the same funding limits, campaign controls, Saturday-Sunday voting period, and other provisions for elections described later in this chapter.

Amendment 1 (pp. 118–19) is a discussion draft of a constitutional amendment to accomplish these goals.

2. Control must be established over campaign contributions, use of television, and length of campaigns. Campaigns are fabulously expensive, and getting more so all the time. One important reason why efforts to limit such spending have failed is that the Supreme Court has held that contributing money to political campaigns is a form of constitutionally protected free speech. Another reason is that legislators and other elected officials naturally want to protect their particular sources of funding and almost never vote to shut off their own contributions.

The big winners are the direct mail industry, television and other advertising media, and the growing army of high-paid consultants—and certainly not the people in terms of useful information. Counting only the visible, reported dollar expenditures (not hidden ones, or the probably larger in-kind contributions), congressional elections cost in the low millions and senatorial elections in the many millions; presidential elections range into the hundreds of millions. To raise such sums, parties and candidates must essentially sell themselves to the highest bidders. And, of course, they do.

The most expensive necessity of campaigning in most areas is access to television, the costs and importance of which seem to escalate together. A second source of the growing expense of campaigns is their increasing length. Any effort to control cam-

{ Discussion Draft }
Amendment 1

Section 1. Notwithstanding any other provision of this Constitution or amendments thereto, all major issues of policy of the
U.S. government shall be referred to the people for decision at
elections held on the Saturday and Sunday of the first full weekend in the months of January, April, July, and October each year.

"Major" issues are those so defined by majority vote of
either house of Congress. But on petition by citizens equal to 5
percent of those voting in the last general election, any issue
before Congress or acted on in the 30 days preceding the filing of
the petition shall be so defined. All "petitions" referred to in this
article shall be in the form, including electronic forms, as Congress may prescribe.

Section 2. The attorney general, guided by the recommenda-
tions of Congress, shall certify the language of the ballot title
and the description of the major components of the issue, as well
as prepare a description of the proposed law's effect on present

paign costs should therefore address not only the amount and
sources of contributions but also access to television and the
length of campaigns.

We propose to limit strictly the money that individuals (including candidates) or corporations can contribute to either candidates or parties or "issue campaigns," to perhaps $100 per
year. At the same time we would require, as a condition of their
licenses to use the public airwaves, that television stations provide a specified amount of free time equally distributed among
parties and candidates qualifying for the ballot. This requirement would apply only to limited times before primaries and
general elections, perhaps sixty days in both cases. Public subsidies could replace some share of the television stations' provable

law, as soon as practical after referral by Congress or such petition is filed. The election provided in Section 1 shall not be scheduled for less than 60 days after the attorney general releases this text to the public. Members of Congress shall have power to append brief statements of views to accompany this text.

Section 3. At any time, on petition by citizens equal to 10 percent of those voting at the last general election, specific proposed legislation included on the petition may be made the subject of the major issue procedure outlined above.

Section 4. The president shall have no veto power with respect to the decisions and/or legislation approved by the people under this article.

Section 5. Congress shall be bound by the intent of the people as expressed under this article. In all other respects, the powers of Congress shall remain unchanged.

Section 6. Congress and the people shall have power to implement the provisions of this article.

losses, and public support could be provided for qualified parties and candidates as a substitute for some share of their campaign expenses. Alternatively, television coverage of all kinds could simply be prohibited—a more radical solution and one that might be constitutionally vulnerable.

Campaigns must be shorter to make these other restrictions effective. Parties and candidates would not be limited as to their fund-raising and planning efforts, but they could not engage in overt campaigning prior to two months before the primary or three months before the general election, whichever was applicable to their case.

Amendment 2 (p. 120) presents a discussion draft of a constitutional amendment to accomplish all these goals.

{ Discussion Draft }
Amendment 2

Section 1. No individual person, corporation, or other entity shall contribute more than $100 to any single party, candidate, campaign committee, issue campaign, or other political cause or purpose, or more than $300 to any combination of the above, in any one year. The Federal Elections Commission shall have power to investigate, prosecute, and/or void elections for violation of this section.

Section 2. Television and radio stations that hold licenses from the U.S. government to use the public airwaves shall, as a condition of such licenses, make free time available at various hours including 7 to 10 P.M. local time on an equal basis to all parties and candidates qualifying for the ballot in state and federal elections. This requirement applies only within 60 days of primary and general elections. In cases where this require-ment imposes special hardship on such stations, they may apply to the Federal Elections Commission for public subsidies.

Section 3. No candidate, party, campaign committee, issue campaign, or other political cause or purpose, shall engage in overt campaigning prior to 60 days before a primary election or 90 days prior to a general election. Overt campaigning shall be defined as distribution of information about issues or candidates, public appearances by or on behalf of candidates or issues, and use of television or radio or print media in any advocacy manner.

Section 4. Congress and the people shall have power to im-plement the provisions of this article.

3. *Proportional voting must be implemented for both federal and state elections.* Proportional voting is a system by which parties or candidates are elected in the same proportions as they win percentages of the vote in multimember-district elections. A party or candidate with 30 percent of the vote in a state with ten electoral college ballots or seats in Congress, for example, would receive 30 percent (or three, in this case) of the ballots or seats at stake. In today's system, such a party or candidate would win *nothing* if another party got 31 percent of the vote and the rest were evenly divided; or it could win *all* in the event that no other party or candidate received more than 29 percent of the vote. In both these last cases, the elected representatives would *all* be representing a minority of less than one-third of the people, and more than two-thirds of the people would be unrepresented and probably unheard.

The purpose of proportional voting—for which there are many possible implementing forms—is to ensure that the actual range of preferences on the part of the voters is reflected in the elected body. Proportional voting helps motivate parties and candidates to distinguish themselves in terms of their issue positions, and it encourages the rise of multiple parties to refine and articulate distinctive issue positions. The result for voters is a wider range of possible options at an election, a wider set of issue preferences in the legislative body, and a more accurate reflection of the actual opinions and preferences of the constituency.

With respect to the presidency, electoral college ballots from the various states should be divided as closely as possible according to the percentages that the various presidential candidates win in each state. Some states are already doing this, and others are considering it. If no candidate receives 40 percent or more of the electoral ballots, there should be a runoff election between the two highest vote gatherers not more than two weeks after the first round of elections.

With respect to Congress, each state with two to five seats in the House of Representatives should institute statewide proportional voting for those seats. States with six or more seats may, at their discretion, establish two intrastate regions with seats allocated according to relative population, within which proportional voting will determine the election of delegates; if they prefer, such states may provide for statewide proportional voting.

With respect to the states, each state must determine for itself how it wishes to implement some form of proportional voting for its legislature. Large states, for example, might want to elect some representatives from geographic districts and others on a proportional basis; or they could elect some from party lists and some on a direct candidate basis. The possible forms of effective proportional voting are almost infinite, and all are fairer to the voters than single-member districts with plurality elections. States should also be encouraged to provide ways that county and city multimember offices will be filled through proportional voting so that the experience with issue prominence over candidates is sunk deeply into the electoral politics of the country.

With respect to issues presented to the voters, ways of weighting preferences or breaking issues into components and posing choices between them might be sought. The issue-decision process might then have two or more stages, in which options are progressively narrowed and popular control maximized.

4. *Multiple parties must be encouraged, and the death grip of the two current major parties destroyed.* The one thing that the Democratic and Republican parties can agree on is that there should never be other parties on the ballot. They have shaped the laws of most states to make it very difficult for other parties to qualify to be on the ballot and to survive between elections. All such laws should be eliminated so that candidacy and ballot access is completely open to all—of whatever party or preference.

The Democrats and Republicans have monopolized our politics for so long that they have very nearly succeeded in making themselves appear to be the very definition of political choices and the full range of alternatives. By any standard of available alternatives, this is absurd. Moreover, both parties are today instruments of domination by financial and other elites. They have served whatever purpose they may once have had, and should now be left to the archives of history.

The time and energy required trying to reform the major parties from within cannot be justified when alternatives are far more efficiently created from without. A multiparty system, furthermore, provides options that embody affirmative choice and preference, rather than the strictly limited, lesser-evil, throw-the-incumbents-out behavior that is the only action allowed by a two-party system. Instead of many small parties, individuals might be able to develop broad enough followings to serve the same purposes.

Proportional voting will help encourage multiple parties, as will encouragement of more independent attitudes in politics. Emphasis on issue-based politics will converge and support both these tendencies. But the vital ingredient will be the determination of ordinary citizens to recover control of their politics and their country, and recognition that the old parties are a major —if not *the* major—impediment to this goal.

There is already encouraging movement in this direction, evident in the 1992 election and still at work today. A major effort to understand the relationship between middle-class attitudes and independent voting was undertaken by Stanley Greenberg after the 1992 elections. His *Middle Class Dreams* offers insight into the dynamics of the three-way vote that gave Ross Perot the highest independent vote in eighty years. Using a large number of standard questions designed to probe reasons for electoral choices, followed by correlation analysis (see the bibliographic essay), Greenberg identified five distinctive attitudinal dimensions:

> *Middle-class consciousness:* a sensitivity to middle-class grievances; a belief that a well-behaved and industrious middle class gets a raw deal, particularly as the poor and others use special claims to get around the rules and gain advantage.
>
> *Anti-government:* a feeling that you cannot trust the government to do the right thing and not screw things up; a belief that politicians are corrupt.
>
> *Anti-establishment:* a belief that the system rewards those

who get around the rules and that public officials and corporations are indifferent to the public interest.

Secular: a belief that government should be tolerant of different views and lifestyles and that government should not interfere with abortion.

Financial pressure: a sense of economic distress, particularly the inability to keep up with prices and make ends meet.

These five sets of attitudes were effective in distinguishing voters for the three candidates and particularly for understanding the distinctive beliefs of the independents. Perot voters (half

declared independents, half drawn equally from Democrats and Republicans) stood out from both other sets in terms of their alienation from government and from all other institutions of the society. They scored particularly high on each of the first three dimensions above. They were also high and in sharp contrast with Bush voters on the secular tolerance dimension. With respect to abortion, they were indistinguishable from Clinton supporters. Above all, they wanted a capable, efficient government that could deliver what people needed in the way of services. They stood for radical change, but not for change that destroyed the capabilities of the government.

With 38 percent of the electorate now identifying themselves as independents, more than identify with either party, the independents such as the Perot voters appear to hold the key to the electoral future. Although they joined in rejecting the Democratic Congress in 1994, they remained profoundly antiestablishment and economic populist in orientation. And they are far more libertarian and secular than Republicans. As Greenberg points out, they are—and by extension, perhaps most independents also will be—unassimilable by *either* political party. If so, the middle class might find its own political voice and no longer be the captive of the established parties and their financial elite sponsors.

5. *Voting options must be increased in various ways.* To enable more citizens to vote, two simple changes should be made. One is to eliminate registration requirements entirely but authorize substituting electronic identification (by Social Security number, or in any number of other ways) for state and local jurisdictions that feel threatened by the prospect of voting fraud by their citizens.

The other is to move the November election from the first Tuesday after the first Monday to the first full weekend of the month. A two-day Saturday-Sunday voting period, instead of a single workday, will maximize opportunities for people to vote. Because of this increased voting period, and because of the drastically shortened campaigns, absentee balloting should be limited to citizens actually out of town, plus the elderly or physically impaired, and then require postmarks within three days prior to the actual voting weekend. With campaigns shortened, it is important that voters delay their decisions until all sides have had an opportunity to make their best case.

Another way to increase voting options is to require that a "None of the Above" (NOTA) option be included on the ballot for every federal and state office to be filled in a general election. If voters feel that all candidates are unqualified or undesirable, or if they simply want to leave the office unfilled, they should have a means of saying so. When a plurality of voters chooses the NOTA option, the election is voided and a new election, with new candidates, shall be scheduled ninety days later; the incumbent will retain his or her office until a successor is certified. If a plurality of voters chooses NOTA a second time, the office could be abolished or its duties merged with those of another office.

Amendment 3 (pp. 127–28) presents a discussion draft of a constitutional amendment to accomplish these goals.

Governance Functions

Our goal is to decentralize, reallocate, and redesign the functions of governments, particularly the central government, with two purposes in mind. The first is to make governance more flexible and more responsive to the people than it is now. The second is to break or at least greatly dilute, by forcing relocation to fifty state capitals, the grip of the financial and other special interests that are so dominant in Washington, D.C. Our proposals are organized in three groups reflecting our three goals; they are illustrative, rather than comprehensive.

Decentralization

Most federal government departments and agencies operate through regional offices in ten designated regions across the country. These regional offices are directed by and report to a central headquarters in Washington, D.C. The extent and effec-

{ Discussion Draft }
Amendment 3

Section 1. Selection by the states of delegates to the electoral college shall be on a proportional basis, i.e., the total number of such delegates from each state shall be apportioned according to the percentages of the statewide vote received by each presidential candidate.

Section 2. In states with from two to five representatives, all members shall be elected by a statewide proportional system that the state shall choose. In all states with six or more representatives, the state shall establish two regions of its choice and elect representatives on a proportional system of its choice within each region.

Section 3. All states shall design appropriate proportional representation systems of their choosing for state legislative office. After five years from the ratification of this article, this provision shall be subject to the jurisdiction of the appropriate state supreme court.

Section 4. All state laws that limit access to the ballot by new or minority parties and candidates, except for those minimal criteria required for financial and legal responsibility, shall be void

tiveness of control exercised from headquarters varies with the department, but standardization of policy and practice is always an important goal of the organization.

One form that decentralization could take is drastically to reduce the size of the headquarters contingent and pass all but the highest administrative responsibilities on to the regions. Regional administrators, armed with broad new discretionary powers and augmented staff, would be accountable in two ways. The first would be to the cabinet secretary or agency head in Wash-

and of no effect. All preferment of the Republican or Democratic parties shall similarly be void and of no effect.

Section 5. There shall be no requirement for citizens to register prior to being entitled to vote in federal or state elections. But states or local jurisdictions with special concern for fraud by their citizens may impose identification requirements, by Social Security number or in some other convenient manner not effectively preventing citizens' right to vote.

Section 6. The November general election for federal and state offices shall be held on the first full Saturday-Sunday weekend of November in applicable years. Absentee ballots must be postmarked within three days of the Saturday voting day.

Section 7. In every election for federal or state office, there shall be included as an option for voters a "None of the Above" (NOTA) opportunity. When a plurality of voters chooses such option, the election shall be voided and a new election required with new candidates after 90 days have elapsed. States may make provision for procedures if NOTA receives a plurality a second time. In the case of federal elections, the office shall remain vacant as to that constituency.

Section 8. Congress and the people shall have power to implement the provisions of this article.

ington, D.C. The second would be to a policy council made up of representatives of the states of the region, chosen as those states might decide (by any number of appointment processes, for example, or by elections).

Another and not necessarily competing form that decentralization could take is simply to move the headquarters of the department or agency out of Washington, D.C., to a major city associated with that function. For example, the Department of the Interior could move to Denver, or the Department of Agriculture to Des Moines, or Labor to Detroit. With today's communications capabilities, there is no reason to mass every department in one city. Minimal staffs in Washington, D.C., could fully serve the informational needs of elected officeholders.

The only departments whose headquarters should remain in Washington, D.C., are State, Defense, Treasury, the CIA, and Justice—functions with external orientation or with roles requiring physical links to the president, Congress, or the Supreme Court. Even here, some functions are already regionalized, and undoubtedly more could be. There are U.S. attorneys for federal judicial districts, for example, and the FBI operates through regional offices.

Secondary benefits from decentralization would be the transfer of good jobs to other areas of the country and reduced pressure for increased salaries and benefits as a result of the lower wage levels and cost of living outside Washington, D.C. But in every case the primary purposes would be well served: greater flexibility and responsiveness to the people, and removal from the dominance of special interests. To the extent that such special interests might simply split their lobbying efforts between the new headquarters and Washington, at least those efforts would become more difficult and more expensive.

Reallocation

By reallocation, we mean rethinking the division of labor between the federal and state governments and the complete transfer of several functions from the federal to the state governments. The federal government has steadily acquired and/or exercised great influence and control over several functional areas ever since the New Deal of the 1930s. Education, housing, welfare, health, and transportation are all examples.

There are several reasons for this, some of which no longer apply or could be corrected: (1) the states were outmoded, incompetent, or seriously biased as governments; (2) the states were very different in levels of population, development, and wealth, so their service levels varied dramatically; (3) states competed with one another to attract and keep businesses and jobs and therefore were unable or unwilling to tap all the potential revenue sources within their borders; and (4) the federal government, partly because it covered the whole country and thus was not subject to the latter limitation, but also because it held power to tax in less visible ways and was more distant from taxpayer reactions, was a far better engine of revenue raising.

But the states have modernized substantially, have abandoned their roles as defenders of segregation and other biases, and may be much more competent and responsive to local differences than the federal government ever could be. The states are still quite different in terms of population, development, and wealth, but their diversity is seen more in terms of strength and less as a liability. Moreover, federal formulas for program improvement or revenue distribution routinely take these differences into account and compensate for them.

The last two reasons given earlier for the growth of centralized influence and control could be corrected by simply letting the federal government impose taxes on a national scale. Using some appropriate distributional formula, the revenues raised could then be passed directly to the states for their discretionary use. In other words, there are no structural impediments to transferring internal functions to the states, if there are otherwise good reasons for doing so.

Education, housing, environmental protection, and welfare seem like good candidates for complete devolution to the states, provided new funding is made available. A larger share of health care and transportation could be included also, but some harmonized national standards are needed in these areas, so the feds should stay relatively more involved. Social Security should remain a federal function.

When devolving existing functions, the federal government could pass that amount of existing revenues to the states to do the jobs involved. The federal government could also impose new taxes, such as import duties or a special per-gallon excise on gasoline (for the additional reasons of controlling pollution and weaning the United States away from imported oil) and pass these revenues to the states for their completely discretionary use.

The states might also develop, perhaps with the aid of pre-agreement to an interstate compact on the part of Congress, a coordinated or common tax system. This would reduce destructive tax competition between them and help the poorer states raise tax revenues. Uniform state corporate income taxes, or value-added taxes, instead of retail sales taxes, are good possibilities.

Redesign

Some governance functions performed at both federal and state levels are simply not working adequately any more. Perhaps most prominent among these are in the judicial system, broadly defined. First, the clogged courts complicate dispute resolution and assert an undesirable policy role. Second, legions of lawyers cut deeply into the productive capabilities of the economy and the fabric of the society.

The courts must be cut back, both in the volume of their caseload and the scope and assertiveness of their jurisdiction. Requirements for mediation or arbitration, limitations on causes of action or rights to jury trial in noncriminal cases, new responsibilities to be borne by plaintiffs, and new powers for judges to speed up pretrial and trial proceedings ought to be enacted. Multiplying the number of judges, the usual solution to crowded court dockets, is both costly and unsatisfactory. Instead, the dockets must be drastically reduced.

Given the greater popular role in policymaking, much of the public policy world ought to be insulated from judicial jurisdiction, leaving only individual constitutional rights as a basis for court action. Congress already has the power to define and limit federal court jurisdiction and should use it aggressively.

But the greatest limitations should be focused on lawyers. In *Facing Up: Paying Our Nation's Debt and Saving Our Children's Future,* Paul Peterson sums up our situation very well:

Americans have become far and away the most litigious people in history. With 5 percent of the world's population, we have 70 percent of its lawyers. Japan has just 11 attorneys for every

100,000 inhabitants, England 82, and Germany 111. We have 281. Americans now file about 18 million lawsuits per year.... In federal courts, filings have nearly doubled since 1970 and tripled since 1960. By some estimates, about 90 percent of all civil lawsuits in the entire world are filed in the United States.

What can possibly explain these stark contrasts? Is this a measure of the breakdown and conflict orientation of our society? It cannot be a sign of health or of the true level of injuries inflicted by individuals among us, unless we are unique in that respect as well. The costs to our economy and society are staggering. Peterson continues:

[C]ompared with Great Britain, a country with similar common-law heritage, the overall cost of tort claims in the United States totals ten times more per capita, the cost of malpractice claims thirty to forty times more, and the cost of product liability claims a hundred times more.

Peterson goes on to point out that the total cost of the U.S. tort system comes to about 2.6 percent of our GNP, five times that of other major industrial countries and the equivalent of all our investment in commercial research and development. Insurance costs can balloon the price of many products and destroy their competitiveness: such costs now account for 5 percent of a new car, half the cost of a football helmet, and 95 percent of a flu vaccine.

There are remedies. We could restrict damage awards, particularly punitive damages, and make them more fully subject to judicial reduction. We could reintroduce notions of comparative liability among defendants (pay only to the extent that you were part of the cause of the damages) and, for plaintiffs, contributory negligence (your damages are limited to the extent that you were a cause of what happened). These changes would help reduce awards to fairer levels.

But the numbers of lawyers seeking income, and the incentives that are available to them, are also part of the problem. American society and culture seem to generate a tragic fascination with the profession of law, perhaps as a misdirected search for justice. Every year, thousands of our best college graduates, who elsewhere would be engineers or scientists or teachers or business innovators, choose instead to seek admission to law schools. The legal curriculum emphasizes individualism, self-interest, and acquisitive materialism; nor can our vast oversupply of lawyers be absorbed in socially constructive occupations, even if that were their preference on graduation.

We might hope that the renewal of economic opportunity and popular control of government would change the present pattern of postcollege choice. But until that time of natural shrinkage in the armies of lawyers, we should consider more formal ways of limiting admission to the bar (or at least to federal court practice), reducing or eliminating contingency fees so that lawsuits are not initiated as a speculative investment, or requiring judges to oversee lawyers' fees and limit them to a provable hourly maximum.

Amendment 4 (p. 134) presents a discussion draft of a constitutional amendment to accomplish goals described here that are not already within the reach of new federal statutes.

Summary

The political class remains in denial, but the people know that the heart of the American problem today lies in the failure of the political system itself—that system of republican government created in 1787 and adapted subsequently to become "representative democracy" by the twentieth century. This is not the first time, of course, that Americans have felt that their political system was captured by self-interested manipulators. A century ago, first Populists and then Progressives asserted that corporations, the wealthy, and political machines were corrupting our politics. The answer to the apparent failures of representative democracy then was a series of innovations, particularly in western states, that instituted a number of "direct democracy" reforms: the initiative, referendum, recall, and direct primary.

For much of the twentieth century, there was debate among

{ Discussion Draft }
Amendment 4

Section 1. Courts in both the federal and state systems must consider the macroeconomic and social implications of their decisions, rather than just the rights of the parties under a single set of facts. Comparative liability and contributory negligence are factors to be considered in both systems.

Section 2. Judges in both federal and state court systems shall have power to review the awards made by juries and the fees charged by lawyers, and set them aside where they are deemed excessive.

Section 3. Congress shall have power to set limits on and prescribe procedures for admission to practice in the federal courts. The intent of this section is to reduce the role of litigation as a means of decision making in the United States.

Section 4. Congress and the people shall have power to implement these provisions.

scholars and others, but most people endorsed both representative and direct democracy. Initiatives and referendums, particularly regarding new constitutions or constitutional amendments, were familiar practices in many states. Representative democracy was always accepted as the dominant mode of crafting everyday legislation and was preferred by the political class. But with growing recognition of the corruption of the political parties and the representative system by money and media, initiatives and referendums have been used with increasing frequency. In 1992 and 1994, there were more initiatives on the ballot in various states than in any year since 1932, and the initiatives of those two years alone represent more than 21 percent of all initiatives in the entire twentieth century.

However, the debate as to whether direct or representative democracy is preferable, or which should be paramount, is false and misleading. The fact is that *both* forms are deeply flawed, and *neither* is free of the corrupting dominance of special interests, their big money, and the media they can buy. Initiatives are increasingly sponsored by wealthy special interests, placed on the ballot by armies of paid signature gatherers, and made the subject of hugely expensive campaigns; moreover, they create a single-issue politics often made up of minor or poorly drafted issues that confuse and deflect voters and end up in extended litigation. They have lost the democracy-expanding roles with which they started. But the standard representative system is, if anything, in even worse shape—for the reasons we have described.

Direct Democracy and Representative Democracy: A Twenty-first-Century Version

Both sides of this supposed dichotomy must be totally reconstructed and made mutually supportive in order to bring the American political system to twenty-first-century viability. Direct democracy can be made deliberative and practical, representative democracy can be genuinely representative and solution-oriented, and the system can be protected against dominance by wealth, parties, and media. In short, the people *can* reclaim control of our system and establish a politics of issues and accommodation.

Earlier, we argued for a "regular referendum" procedure in which all major issues would be framed for popular decision by a nonpartisan source, which would be responsible for circulating to the voters an objective analysis of current law, proposed changes, and arguments for and against it. At quarterly intervals, after a minimum of 60 days for discussion and debate, decisions on a set of four or five such issues would be made by all eligible voters, with balloting by mail, in person, and perhaps by electronic means, over an extended weekend period. The general framework and basic substance of the voters' decision would be binding on Congress, which would nevertheless retain the significant task of shaping the issues and arguments for voter decision and subsequent statutory and regulatory implementation of those decisions.

At the same time, a form of proportional representation would be instituted by eliminating the single-member district system of forced choice between one Democrat and one Republican for each open seat in the legislature. Instead, all candidates would run at large on the basis of personal platforms reflecting their values and beliefs. Voters would have first, second, and third preferences recorded for allocation and reallocation of their votes as the candidates with the lowest vote totals are progressively eliminated until all open seats are filled. The result will be a legislative body reflecting the full range of voter opinion in which political parties play little or no role, and each voter knows that he or she is represented by a specific legislator with views most like his or her own. The legislator knows that he or she must deliver on behalf of those like-thinkers or face rejection at the next election. Negotiation among legislators can be based on rational win-win problem solving (within the framework of voter-set directions) instead of party or campaign contributor preferences.

The point of these changes is to solve the problems that are too visible on each side today, make the contenders complementary to each other, and generate a new and truly *deliberative* democracy. This synthesized direct *and* representative version must be protected against big money in the long run by constitutional amendment authorizing effective limits on excessive campaign contributions and mandating short campaign periods. Until then, rigorous reporting requirements with severe penalties for delay or violation must be imposed by federal and state statutes. Similarly, until appropriate amendments are in place, federal statute can require more equal access to TV time in shortened campaign periods.

The political class will raise objections to the changes proposed, particularly to the necessity of making several of them through amendments to the U.S. Constitution. We respond first that the voters know all too well that the system has been captured by special interests and self-interested opportunists; they are determined to reclaim it for themselves, and these changes are the minimum means necessary. Second, we remember that when change is necessary, it can be accomplished quickly and decisively: the original Constitution, with all its radical innovations, was ratified in a mere nine months under the communications and transportation conditions of 1787–88—and the Twenty-sixth Amendment in only three months in 1972! Of course, there is reason to try the new deliberative democracy in several states prior to instituting it at the national level, but other delaying tactics should not be tolerated. Voter confidence in the American political system cannot be restored in any other way than by moving promptly to institute the new deliberative democracy.

The Last Laugh, by Fernando Krahn. *The Atlantic,* October 1972. Reprinted by permission of HWLA, Inc., agent for the illustrator. Copyright © 1972 by Fernando Krahn.

SIX

The New American Democracy

"Lots to cover in this last session, folks," David warned as they all settled in the living room after dinner. "We need to get quickly from how it all happened to how you felt at the time to what you think today about what was most important. From the Declaration on the Fourth of July, 2000, to the ratification of all four of the constitutional amendments took about five years."

"Five years, three months and twelve days for the last and biggest of them," Mary interrupted quietly.

"And then the economic program came on line in another couple of years," David went on imperturbably. "That's a heck of a lot of basic change in the space of only seven or eight years! What did people *do* to bring it all about?"

"David, lots of different people did lots of different things," Jeff said patiently. "Everybody understood that it was simply not possible to have some kind of specific blueprint. What we had was the sense of absolute necessity in the face of the economic collapse and a desperate kind of faith and trust in one another. We knew the basic goals because they were set forth in the Declaration. We knew our immediate objectives because they were set out in the constitutional amendments.

"But we were facing long odds—at best a one-in-ten chance of winning—and people had to do what made sense under the circumstances to implement passage of the amendments by Congress and then get ratification in the states. There were lots of different strategies and tactics used by different parts of the movement, depending on the special situations in their districts and states. Essentially, people simply had to trust one another and hope for the best!"

"My favorite tactic was to argue with people about the economic program," Mary said smugly. "And when they agreed that we needed jobs, income, fairness, and decent trade and fiscal policy, I would ask them why they couldn't just enact them? I got all kinds of explanations, and pretty soon people started looking sheepish and saying, well, why can't we? Let's do it! And then we'd start talking about how to do it, and who was in the way, and how to get around them."

"So you were really bringing people to the support of the four constitutional amendments, Mom?" asked David.

"Of course," Mary replied. "But that was only the beginning. Then we had to organize and pressure Congress—meaning every single representative and senator in his or her home district or state—to enact the amendments and pass them on to the states. Then we had to do the same kind of pressure building on state legislatures to ratify them."

Jeff leaned back with a smile. "Now *that* was creativity time! Our folks developed different tactics in different parts of the country, and it was like, who could be more imaginative in getting their legislatures to ratify the amendments? We had tax refusals, sit-ins at legislative hearings and sessions, local boycotts of businesses that opposed us, even general strikes—everything that made clear to the legislatures that we were a determined majority. Sometimes we had demonstrations, but they were dangerous because the establishment could always send in provocateurs or create incidents that made us look bad."

David's face showed his concern. "How much violence was there? I mean, it's just not possible that changes of this significance could be accomplished totally peacefully—some big corporations and really wealthy people and a lot of professionals were going to have to give up their advantages, and nobody does that kind of thing willingly. I mean, I know that lots of advocates of change just talk about change as if it doesn't matter what the *content* of the change is. And even more seem to think that if they just whisper in the ears of the people in power, those people will fundamentally change their ways without a second thought. But you were seeking real, fundamental change in both the structure of power *and* the basic policies of the country—and you had already *shown* what a difference you wanted to make in the country. Lots of other alternatives were being urged in the midst of the economic crisis. You *had* to face opposition!"

Mary stood up and circled the room thoughtfully. "Your analysis, and your question, are right on target, David. But I guess that, overall, and considering the scope of change in seven or eight years, you'd have to call it a nonviolent process. There were three or four violent incidents, with a few people injured and a couple killed. And there were some scary confrontations, where worse things might have happened. By comparison with the everyday violent crime rate of the times, however, this was practically nothing.

"What mattered was that we always were careful to show our numbers somehow—to make clear that we were both a thoughtful and a decisive majority and therefore entitled to act in that situation. We acted always in the name of democracy, and we played by the rules and won offices and were often the legitimate officials with legal public authority, which meant that law-enforcement people almost had to be on our side. The opposition had trouble making itself appear to have a better claim to power than we did, and therefore they were on the defensive."

David shook his head, still wondering how ordinary people found the courage and determination to mount a ten-year campaign to take back their government. "Did you *know* what you were doing?" he finally blurted out.

"You mean did we think we were making history?" Jeff asked, laughing. "Mostly we didn't have time to think, but yes, once we got started, we had some pretty grand hopes and we wanted them to come true and we knew that if they did, it would mean that we would be different and the country would be different. So I suppose you could say that we had a sense of making history."

"No," Mary said flatly. "We did what we had to one day after another, and when it was all over—," she paused. "Actually, it's not over yet, but there was a point after several years when people started to look back and marvel at how far we had come. History is of course made by numbers of people rather than by great heroes, but not consciously or quite how they intend. And often they don't really know they're doing it."

David frowned and tried to regain direction of the interview. "You sound as if you are disagreeing, but I think you're actually saying the same thing. Just tell me the one thing you were thinking most strongly while everything was under way. Dad, go first?"

"OK," Jeff responded. "For me, it was the overwhelming sense of the need for tangible achievements. We needed substance to focus on, to rally around, and to organize to get enacted or whatever. The four constitutional amendments were even better than the Declaration because they embodied our economic and political program. We had to push each one of them, first in Congress as it was and then in every one of the states. Each one gave us something specific to argue for, and each passage gave us new determination."

So much for the man who stands for vision and process over program, thought David. But he said, "And you, Mom?"

Mary rocked slowly and smiled at him, as if reading his thoughts and enjoying the prospect of complicating his analysis still further. "For me it was the incredible uncertainty about everything. You couldn't count on anything, and there was no such thing as a blueprint or clear strategy that you could follow. It was all chaos and confusion, with terrible alternatives looking more likely most of the time.

"I remember a line that we used over and over again. It came from Anna Louise Strong, in a newspaper article just before the Seattle General Strike of 1919. That was the first general strike in American history, when everybody just stopped working and the labor unions ran the city. Because it came soon after the Russian Revolution of 1917, it seemed that the United States was about to erupt in revolution, and everybody was scared. Anna Louise Strong was a powerful female voice at a time when women weren't much up-front in politics, and she said, 'We are undertaking the most tremendous move ever made . . . in this country, a move which will lead—NO ONE KNOWS WHERE!'

"You could just feel people start to shake when that line came out! It appealed to us powerfully, whenever we started calling for boycotts or demonstrations or general strikes to crank up the pressure on state legislatures to ratify the constitutional amendments—and it sure scared them!"

"Good." David was determined to be unflappable now and do his analysis from his notes later. "And what's the strongest memory that you have today about those years? What's the lesson for history that you would offer?"

"Easy," Jeff said quickly. "It's what it feels like to move from being totally passive and acted upon to being fully active and part of a huge group of people, all in motion together and making things happen. It's the change in yourself as this happens, in every aspect of how you see and think about the world around you and who you are in it. And the difference in the country as this happened to millions of individuals within a pretty short period of say, eight or ten years."

"Yes," Mary joined with alacrity. "What I see now is how ready everybody was for this incredible turnaround from passive to active. In the 1990s, it looked like the middle class would be passive forever, except for the rise of independent voters, some taxpayer revolts, and other scattered protests. And then all of a sudden the whole world was in motion, doing things you couldn't have imagined only a couple of years earlier. They had to have been ready all along, and just waiting for a spark!"

David's admiration showed clearly on his face, together with a touch of yearning to have been part of the drama of those times. Then he remembered his assignment and held up his hand. "One last question, happy warriors. Tell me the single most important step, or part of your program, that your movement accomplished in that whole time."

David looked from Jeff to Mary with his pencil poised, anticipating another lively disagreement. Instead, his parents smiled warmly at each other, each inviting the other with body language to speak for the two of them.

"We *know* the answer to that one, David, because we've talked about it a lot," Mary said confidently. "Nothing compares with the impact of the direct democracy amendment, the one that put all major issues up for decision by the national electorate four times every year. With it, everything came together and all our problems became soluble. Without it, we probably would have ended up with the same failed representative system that big money and the old political parties dominated, to say nothing about losing the economic program because the old power structure wouldn't allow it."

"That's right," Jeff exclaimed, half out of his chair. "Multiple parties and proportional voting were a big help, but the principle that the people would vote directly on all major issues just reverberated throughout the whole society and set off a series of changes that really transformed us *and* the country! We didn't even realize all its implications when we first started advocating it—and of course everybody who knew anything about politics laughed or sneered at us for being so simple-minded as to think the people could be trusted actually to make decisions.

"But when Vermont began its two-year experiment using the procedures of our proposed amendment, and Minnesota and Colorado started up three-year experiments, we began to understand how it changed *everything,* not just who made decisions. It was the glue that united our movement and at the same time the solvent that began to reduce or eliminate each of the major problems facing the country! Think about it! Both glue and solvent!"

David was having trouble keeping up, with the facts and with the metaphors that so appealed to his father. "Dad, I'm getting lost! Can you do it one step at a time?"

Mary smiled and took over. "Number one. It engaged lots of ordinary voters who never bothered to learn about issues because they never felt that their vote mattered. They studied, and they voted, and they felt a whole new connection with one another and with the government because all of a sudden, and together, they *controlled* what it did. And they took their responsibility seriously and began to vote in larger and larger proportions.

"Number two. It made issues, rather than candidates, important, and it changed our representatives from free agents bought by big money into issue-framing technicians with little or no important discretionary power. It completely bypassed the old political parties, broke their grip on public policy, and made them useless to big money. Ideas, and their capacity to solve problems, became paramount. Multiple parties took off, and a wide variety of proposed solutions was available for every problem.

"Number three. On all major issues, the old power structure became powerless—replaced by the people—without being physically overthrown. The people could therefore enact the economic nationalist program we worked so hard to develop because the corporations and banks and wealthy could no longer block it. We got the tax policy and the fiscal policy and the trade policy that made sense for American workers, not for the financial elite. That elite still felt powerful—after all, it still existed and the rolodexes still produced—but the people ruled as never before.

"Number four. As people focused more and more on their decision making with respect to the major issues, they developed a sense of responsibility—for the long-term common interest, for one another, and for the country as a whole. It was much less individual self-interest or group against group; it was more everybody together. The culture war that had earlier seemed so destructive began to give way to efforts at mutual understanding and consensus building.

"Number five. The more we all engaged in these quarterly national decisions, the more we began to feel different as people. We were in control, we had to be responsible, we had to think about the long-term common interest, and we began to feel new strengths as individual people—we were *citizens* at last! So *this* was what democracy could be! It felt good!"

"Mom, are you a lawyer or a preacher?" David teased as Mary paused for breath.

"Better yet," Jeff said with a grin. "A philosopher would tell you that technological change had made possible something that could not have been imagined in the two-hundred-year past but that became an imperative because it enabled fulfillment of the powerful appeal that democracy embodies. We can implement direct democracy today because of our communications capabilities, and it changes our world and ourselves when we do. If we value democracy, and we can have it in its purest form, why not?"

"Well, I guess some people really don't want it," David demurred, "or they're afraid of what the people might do."

"Of course," Jeff replied. "But do you think the people could do any worse than the politicians did for the thirty years before 2000? At least the people would be paying the price for *their own* mistakes and maybe would learn from them and do better the next time."

"Guess so," David concurred. "I have really learned a lot. Would you like to hear my tentative conclusions?"

"Some other time," Mary said as she reached for Jeff's hand and pulled him out of his chair. "The old folks are going to say good night while they still have some energy left."

"Good night, Mom and Dad, and thanks for everything," David said, jotting quickly in his notebook.

It didn't occur to him to wonder why old folks needed energy to go to bed, or why this discussion might cause them to leave with their arms around each other.

Never has the American prospect seemed more discouraging and never has it been more promising. The implacable forces of economic and technological change are creating precisely the enabling crisis in which the Jeffersonian principles of decentralization, reliance on independent small business and property holders, and popular control of governments at all levels can finally be realized.

The Imminence of the Jeffersonian Transformation

For the first time in our history, the economic and technological context permits, even *mandates,* the modern version of Jefferson's democratic aspirations. Hamiltonian upper-class, big-money, big-government centralization, with all its distance from and insulation against popular impact, is being undermined by contemporary reality. Three primary factors are subverting that system and preparing the way for a new politics of issues, a direct democracy based on periodic votes on major issues.

First, as nineteenth- and early twentieth-century mass production recedes into the past, it takes with it such associated concepts as mass trade unions and mass political parties, the old liberal and conservative ideologies, and, most important for our purposes, representative democracy. Such basic concepts and organizational forms are being transformed or discarded as the transformation proceeds on its relentless course.

For example, the old representative system was appropriate to geographic distinctiveness, slow and difficult communications, limited access to information, and poor transportation. It was designed to keep the bulk of the people *out* of decision making because there appeared no way for them to have adequate knowledge or understanding of issues and problems. When the New Deal and Great Society gave many new powers and functions to the national government, with this deflecting system nevertheless in place, people were effectively excluded from many vital matters affecting them. The result was a learned passivity and distance, which soon enough bred distrust and resentment.

We live in a drastically different world, with less significance to geographic differences, very rapid transportation, great personal mobility, and multiple forms of instantaneous communication and ways of acquiring information. We no longer have to wait for an excited courier to come galloping into town and read us a three-day-old newspaper from Boston, and we need not act as if we do.

No matter how vast the scale of the nation or how widely separated citizens may be, they are greatly empowered by e-mail, internet, teleconferencing, interactive television, on-line services, faxes, telephones, overnight package delivery anywhere, and quick postal service. Communities of interest focused on environmental health and safety issues or the defense of Medicare are already organized, and many others are sure to follow. It is only a short step further to focus analysis and advocacy around such structural change goals as the Declaration and the four constitutional amendments.

Second, there is a vast pool of angry middle-class people—70 million families earning between $25,000 and $100,000 a year, the American bedrock—who have been systematically drained of their economic security, political efficacy, and self-confidence. They are slowly coming to a still-imperfect understanding of the extent of their betrayal by dominant elites and are beginning to recognize the enormity of what has been done to them and their values over the past thirty years. Reconstruction cannot begin until denial stops and is replaced by recognition of the moral entitlement of the middle class to reassert itself in the name of the American future. This is what is happening today: profound distaste for politicians and the old political parties is evolving into a desire for a "do-it-yourself" approach to politics.

The title of a provocative book published in 1995 by Christopher Lasch neatly sums up our premise here: *The Revolt of the Elites and the Betrayal of Democracy*. Lasch says:

To an alarming extent, the privileged classes—by an expansive definition, the top 20 percent—have made themselves independent not only of crumbling industrial cities but of public services in general.... In effect, they have removed themselves from common life.... Many of them have ceased to think of themselves as Americans in any important sense, or implicated in America's destiny for better or worse.

Lasch sees this new financial elite as identifying only with its counterparts in other countries, not with the needs and problems of ordinary Americans. Great polarization of wealth and income, Lasch says, creates a situation where the rulers ignore or deny the values and aspirations of the middle class.

Simultaneously arrogant and insecure, the new elites, the professional classes in particular, regard the masses with mingled scorn and apprehension.... Middle Americans ... are at once absurd and vaguely menacing.... It is the crisis of the middle class, and not simply the growing chasm between wealth and poverty, that needs to be emphasized in a sober analysis of our prospects.... Whatever its faults, middle-class nationalism provided a common ground, common standards, a common frame of reference without which society dissolves into nothing more than contending factions, as the Founding Fathers of America understood so well—a war of all against all.

The simple fact is that middle Americans have nobody to trust but themselves. The U.S. government, controlled by the nation's bipartisan economic and political establishment acting through the two major political parties and their officeholders, has effectively violated its contract with the people and become the agent of a vast upward redistribution of wealth. Doing so, it has lost legitimacy in the eyes of the people, and antigovernment feelings run higher than at any time since 1776.

But the people *need* a capable, powerful, and trustworthy government to act as their agent in correcting this situation and to serve the long-term public interest of the society as a whole. Government itself, *once restored to the control of the people,* must be legitimate in their eyes and supported by them as it works their will. Government is not *inherently* the problem;

who controls government, and for what purposes, are what matters.

The implication is so obvious that even the person who runs can read it: the people must take back their government and control its major actions directly, by themselves and without the "help" of parties or politicians. Jefferson was quite clear on this point in a 1787 letter to Madison:

> And say, finally, whether peace is best preserved by giving energy to the government, or information to the people. This last is the most certain, and the most legitimate engine of government. Educate and inform the whole mass of the people.... On their good sense we may rely with the most security for the preservation of a due degree of liberty.

Third, the two major parties, creaking with their obsolescence in the context of the ongoing economic and social transformation, are fragmenting in advance of self-destructing. Both parties are struggling to hold their factions together, and if one fragments the other is likely to do the same. A plurality of all voters, and a majority of young voters, currently identify themselves as independents. Big money buys individual candidates on the open market, and party loyalties become trivial. Party platforms have *never* been meaningful. The special interests dominate the policymaking process, often with their lobbyists actually writing legislation. The people have no way to affect decisions on major issues.

This is a situation just waiting to topple over from a modest nudge from any number of possible sources. A significant independent party with apparent staying power, or an independent reform movement with broad support, could do the job. A financial crisis triggered by a Third World country's debt repudiation, a monetary failure, or the collapse of a major bank—or a depression brought about in any number of ways—would have the same impact. What appears to some to be the central "given" of American politics is actually a naked emperor fidgeting nervously in his house of cards while watching a video of our modern Rome burning.

A Politics of Issues
through Direct Democracy

The direct democracy proposal we embodied in the first of our proposed constitutional amendments (pp. 118–19) is at the heart of our argument. With it in effect, everything else becomes possible. Without it, the existing power structure, parties, politicians, and special interests remain capable of blocking all reforms not to their liking.

In that amendment, we drew on contemporary initiative and referendum practices in several states to develop a plan for identifying major issues, drafting the form of a ballot question in which two or more alternatives would be posed, giving the voters all necessary information, providing time for debate and reflection, and then enabling a timely choice through quarterly weekend voting opportunities. We envision experiments in several states with procedures varying on this basic model, and refinement based on this experience, before instituting the national version.

Direct democracy so implemented is a practical means for American voters to take back their government and assert control over its basic policies. It does not require or permit people to micromanage everything that government does; no national electorate can or should be expected to do so. But it *does* provide a rewarding focus for sustained political action, and it alone *does* make possible the solution to otherwise apparently intractable obstacles in the way of a successful middle-class revolution.

Direct democracy of this kind provides the glue that holds its supporters together because it offers a clear, dramatic, and very attractive goal on which to focus their energies. This form of direct democracy promises a politics of issues in which the people would finally acquire real power over the basic policies of the national government. It not only expresses their current anger and resentment but also creates a practical mechanism for assuring popular control that bypasses representatives, parties, power structures, and special interests. In short, it offers hope of replacing today's discredited system with a twenty-first-century government by the people.

Many implications flow from the prospect of instituting and working with quarterly national decisions on major issues, and they add up to a kind of solvent for both the obstacles facing a middle-class revolution and the problems facing the country. The experience of working together to achieve ratification of this amendment will itself help to transform people into active, self-confident citizens. People will have a renewed sense of owner-ship and responsibility for the entire political system and once more will begin to think in terms of what we share, rather than what divides us. From the struggle, a whole new sense of social identity and purpose will emerge, and once again Americans will see their country as a model for the world.

After some early experience with quarterly policymaking under these procedures, several other important benefits will be-come visible. An obvious one is that the entire economic nation-alist program will now be possible because all the current barri-ers will have been swept away. *There is no other way that this vital, middle-class-preserving program can be implemented be-cause the existing dominance by corporations, banks, and the wealthy, to say nothing of career politicians, the Democratic and Republican parties, and the assembled special interests, will never permit that economic program to see the light of day.* The grip on Congress exercised by all these entities for so long will be dissolved by direct popular policymaking.

Middle-class values will be revalidated, and middle-class self-confidence will be restored, by the reality of taking back control of the government. The values and beliefs that built this country are not evil, trivial, or fake. There are many ways in which they can be adapted or improved to meet present and future needs, and we have suggested several. But, first, the point must be fully and finally established that the American bedrock has not been wrong in its basic commitments.

Many more subtle effects will be noticeable as the new sys-tem becomes a major tool of civic education. People generally will spend more time understanding issues and will respond more exclusively to the significance of different choices because their votes will now make a difference. Many more people will begin to take part in these quarterly votes because they will be meaningful. We will think more in terms of the common interest and the long term, and about such basic questions as what we want and need the government to do, because now *the government will be us.* The more majoritarian the process and the more we think in terms of what we share, the more the culture war will be muted.

But what if we make a mistake? What if, for example, a popular majority chooses to ban imports from Japan and thereby triggers a trade war? There are several answers. First, it may not be a "mistake" at all, except in the eyes of some who would prefer otherwise. Second, if it is a mistake, it can be corrected by the same procedure by which it was made. Third, the civic education derived from making and correcting a mistake will be valuable.

Fourth, even if the mistake is not corrected, it is better to follow what majorities want than to impose some (equally error-prone) second-guessing, top-down corrective on their judgment. Long-term civic education may be the result, and probably the country will survive the mistake quite well. It certainly has had to survive a substantial number of mistakes made by the power-holders of the last several decades!

But what will be the role of the old power structure, old parties, career politicians, big money, and other special interests after direct democracy cuts through their cozy grip on government? Will they simply disappear? The answer is that they will probably stay in denial for a while and keep right on with business as usual, perhaps hoping to outlast the new reality or find a way to tame and control it. (The obvious route—to use their money and influence to shape the outcome of national issues voting—will be blocked by the new constitutional limits on spending on issues elections.)

To the extent that some expertise and stability are provided by this continuity, it could even be a useful result. Tension between the regularly asserted power of nationalist popular majorities and the self-interest of the internationalist class of financial elites could be constructive. At the least, it would bring the basic character of the American social conflict out in the open and give middle Americans the leverage to manage the transition to a fully global system on their own terms.

The New American Century

Perhaps the greatest achievement to be anticipated from this version of direct democracy is a massive on-the-job education in civic responsibility, leading to the restoration of political self-confidence and purpose among the American middle class. Voters will be obliged to seek consensus rather than conflict, to listen to one another rather than shout past each other, and generally to behave as public citizens rather than as mere cost-benefit calculating taxpayers. We will learn to look forward as a community, and to make choices that are in the long-term common interest. We will emerge with an adapted ideological perspective built around a core of long-standing values, but one that willingly embraces the future. We will be far more satisfied with our lives and confident in our futures.

The new system will enable us to address fully, and act decisively on, problems that have for too long been left to "experts" and self-interested advocates. The balance between economic growth and environmental quality, for example, can now be decided by a relatively objective citizenry with concern for their children's future, rather than short-term corporate profit pressures. The government can always count on the informed support of the majority of its citizens, whatever the tasks it undertakes.

We will all rest secure in the knowledge that it is the general public interest, as best understood by a majority of the voting public, that shapes government action—and not the money, influence, or corruption of special-interest politics. We will have positioned ourselves as a country to act decisively and with a clear sense of our national interest in the international political and economic world.

Most satisfying of all will be the social achievement of making Jeffersonian democracy real in our society and in our personal lives. In Jefferson's version, small business and small property holdings provided the independence that enabled ordinary people to be free and participating members of the society. The economic program is crucial to this setting, and the political program to its efficacy.

But democracy was always demeaned by being understood as social mobility, access to material things, enlightened self-interest, procedural due process, or even tolerance. The new system brings with it the civic education, mutual public respect, and personal political responsibility that add up to civic virtue. Ordinary men and women, taking responsibility to become competent citizens, acting with loyalty to the community and one another, accepting the moral obligation to make self-reliant choices that shape the future, and accepting accountability for their actions—those are the conditions of Jeffersonian democracy. Such civic virtue, not more effective representation or elaborate procedures such as checks and balances, is the proper foundation of democratic life.

With new public energy and sophistication under development, middle Americans will be able to enjoy an entirely new level of public and personal satisfactions. The United States will return to the heights of combined moral and material achievement and will again be the model for the world that we want to be. What appeared in the early 1990s to be inevitable decline and disintegration can become the launching pad for a new century eclipsing all that was ever imagined for our country.

The responsibility for change, therefore, lies with us. We must begin with ourselves, teaching ourselves not to close our minds prematurely to the novel, the surprising, the seemingly radical. This means fighting off the idea-assassins who rush forward to kill any new suggestion on grounds of its impracticality, while defending whatever now exists as practical, no matter how absurd, oppressive, or unworkable it may be. It means fighting for freedom of expression—the right of people to voice their ideas, even if heretical.

Above all, it means starting this process of reconstruction now, before the further disintegration of existing political systems sends the forces of tyranny jackbooting through the streets, and makes impossible a peaceful transition to twenty-first-century democracy.

If we begin now, we and our children can take part in the exciting reconstitution not merely of our obsolete political structures but of civilization itself.

Like the generation of the revolutionary dead, we have a destiny to create.

— Alvin and Heidi Toffler,
Creating a New Civilization

EPILOGUE

David Reynolds's Final Paper, 26 November 2012

Conclusion

I have now presented my findings with respect to my parents' activities and feelings during the 1996–2012 period we are investigating, and it is time for some conclusions. I offer some preliminary impressions and then answer the specific questions of the assignment. From there, I go on to more speculative interpretations and personal reactions to the project from the perspective of my generation.

First, this was a wonderful way to get to know my parents and what makes them tick. Of course I had heard scraps of these stories from time to time, but never in this coherent way, where what they did could be

evaluated in historical as well as personal
terms. They <u>knew</u> they had little chance to
win, but they went out and beat the odds.
They were ordinary people deeply engaged in
a dramatic and sustained collective effort--
and really in the middle of great actions
and achievements that (pardon the cliché)
changed the world! I'm actually a little
jealous of their situation! How many generations have that opportunity, and how many
actually make good on it? How would people
feel today if they had let that opportunity
go by because it was such a long shot?

Second, my dominant reaction is that de-
ciding to commit themselves irretrievably to
accomplishing the goals of the Declaration
and amendments was far more difficult than
actually doing so. The status quo has lit-
erally a million justifications, and people
have a similar number of rationalizations
about why it can never be changed. The understanding of the 1960s as a time of failure seemed to confirm this for lots of
people. Often, people shrink from taking an
unpopular stand or exposing themselves as
advocates of drastic change. It was really
true that the only thing they had to fear
was fear itself.

(<u>Aside to the class:</u> We need to focus explanatory efforts specifically on what enabled our respondents to dislodge themselves from their relatively comfortable--or at least anonymous and noncontroversial--lives, cross the threshold into public advocacy, and thrust themselves into the desperate effort to achieve the goals of the Declaration and amendments. How did they have the courage to withstand the heat from their Nervous Nellie employers, family, friends, and acquaintances? Who else found that their parents just went out and risked everything for their children? That still amazes me.)

The irony in this point is how relatively easy it was to topple the apparently permanent system in place in the 1990s. To coin another phrase, that system was nothing but a paper tiger--already so rotten at the core that it posed only very modest resistance and then gave way to the pressure from below, once it became clear that the pressure was genuinely that of a determined majority. Who could have predicted that? Between the time the revolutionary movement was nothing except the butt of every establishment joke to the time that it was transforming American politics was less than five years.

On to the questions posed in the assignment. On what date did the revolutionary process start? Certainly before the Declaration was approved, because a tremendous organizing effort that engaged millions of people effectively was required to draft and refine it. I would say the revolution started when a critical mass of people became powerfully committed to the goal of fundamental change, and began to find and trust one another in part through the spiritual awakening my parents described. It was only after that point that the flurry of negotiations and communications and drafting of the Declaration actually began. In other words, reaching the general commitment to basic change preceded the specific, articulated version of their goals that were then set forth in the Declaration and amendments. But I agree that historians will date it from the Fourth of July, 2000, because that is such a nice, clear event.

Next, what motivated people, what did they do, and when did they realize what they were doing? I have answered most of this question earlier, and will add just a couple of comments here. Motivations were probably very different among different people, but I think the common denominator is deep and

profound disgust with the way things were
working--or not working. Transforming that
disgust into action is the crucial threshold, and here the spark seems to have been
thinking about the future (indeed, about us,
their children, quite specifically), and
again the spiritual dimension uniting their
little band with others and with the natural
world and generating a determination to make
the world over into what it could be.

What they did sounds simple enough: they
did whatever was necessary to achieve the
goals of the Declaration. This meant,
first, to get the amendments ratified and
then to pass the economic program. Recognition of the implications of what they were
doing really did not come until some time
later because they were too busy dealing
with each day's crises as they came up. But
when they did tumble to what they had done
as ordinary people--really making history--
they were simultaneously humble and proud
(does that make sense?), and they poured all
those feelings into a restored definition of
civic virtue and what it meant to be a
''citizen,'' which they simply acted out instead of describing it in elaborate self-
congratulatory detail.

What was the most important thing they did? Well, obviously it was the direct democracy amendment. What political innovation has ever had a shorter transit from joke to implementation or was ever more appropriate to a society's combination of technological capability and political necessity?

Finally, how did they feel along the way, and were they ever discouraged and afraid of alternatives winning out? I do not think even the most determined activists started out believing that they were going to succeed. They just knew that they had to try, that they could not let their American heritage go down the drain without doing everything possible to prevent it.

They had to have an alternative program because, as my mom never tires of saying, you can't fight something with nothing. But they accepted the fact that there could not be a blueprint for every step along the way, and they recognized that people who asked for a blueprint were unconsciously clinging to the status quo. The Declaration and the amendments were all the specifics they needed; more would have been counterproductive in the same manner as a blueprint.

And the fact is, they were desperately afraid that any number of other results were going to occur. My dad got really excited, generated a double shot of hope, and went roaring off with huge new momentum when he decided that they had a realistic one-in-ten chance of success!

What have we learned about making big changes in the real world? I think the most important requirement in this situation is that you have to go beyond a tolerance for ambiguity (which you certainly need) to actually enjoying uncertainty and the challenge of finding workable responses through trial and error.

What will happen is simply unknowable, but you still have to act, and the courage, decisiveness, and appearance of confidence to do so are crucial qualities.

Next, history and theory probably help some, but not very much. Sometimes they can be constraining rather than empowering. I think everybody was too hung up on what went wrong in the 1960s, and it inhibited some people from getting started at all and others from acting more decisively at times when they should have. The better approach

is to think hard about the future and what
technological and economic conditions will
be like and then design a political strategy
and goals that are appropriate to those prospective conditions. The world is coher-
ent--that is, conditions in different
spheres of social life such as the economy
and cultural values and politics tend to fit
together. Politics lags behind the other
areas. But if you can see what kind of politics would fit with what is happening in
the other areas, then you need to get out
front and adapt that kind of politics to
your goals.

What I really want to talk about in
closing is what this all means for my generation. Essentially, I feel an overpowering
sense of awe and gratitude for what was
risked and accomplished and an absolute determination to see that my generation ful-
fills the opportunities and responsibilities
passed on to us.

First, the people who accomplished these
changes have made it possible for me to have
a quality of life that was becoming unimag-
inable for young adults in the 1990s. I can
actually anticipate a future where things
will mostly improve and where economic

growth and environmental quality will be balanced so that we maintain our biosphere in ways that should make it last forever. I can plan for an economic future that includes buying a decent house, marrying, raising a small family in which the kids can have rising expectations too--things that almost an entire generation of young people in the 1980s and 1990s missed out on. And I know that I can play a real part in shaping everything that happens in my lifetime.

Second, the work of these people essentially restored the social fabric of American life at a time when it looked like it was being irretrievably shredded. Sure, there are differences between people and groups today, but nothing like the 1990s. We have a genuine concern for one another and for the long-term development and improvement of the whole society. If there is a crucial principle that has been brought back, it is that we all--well, most of us-- feel and display a sense of trust. That trust starts in our own capabilities, expands into interpersonal relations, and on to the whole national community. We do not suspect or denigrate one another anymore; we respect and listen to others as never before.

Finally, of all that has been accomplished, I think the most important is the new sense of citizenship and responsibility that I and others like me have acquired. We are inheriting a vastly more promising world that was made possible by the daring gamble and incredible determination of our parents, and we had better make good on what they did for us. That means hard work, self-discipline, and continuing educational effort so that we can be responsible citizens. We need to adapt our values and beliefs and practices continually to the unfolding future so that our economic and political systems work smoothly for all of us. We have to accept the moral obligation of carrying this revitalized civilization forward until we can proudly pass an even better world on to our children. This is the way we can thank our parents for what they achieved on our behalf.

APPENDIX

New Technology,
New Politics?

In this brief appendix, we speculate about the prospective impact on American politics of the rapid growth and development of telecommunications, such as personally controlled interactive television, e-mail, fax machines, the internet, and other decentralized electronic systems. Essentially, we argue that the effects could be as powerfully transformative as the impact of television since 1960, but in the reverse direction. Television focused on the central sources of news and interpretation, giving them unprecedented manipulative power over passive viewers. The new means of telecommunications enable an active citizenry to be in instant communication with like-minded others and develop their own interpretations and preferences. The result could be an equally unprecedented empowerment of rank-and-file movements, many having values and goals fundamentally opposed to the establishment's complacent management of the status quo.

Imagine that you had been asked in January 1950 to forecast the impact of television on American politics. Although many homes were still without TV sets, people generally were already experienced with the medium and its entertainment capabilities. Game shows and the *Ed Sullivan Show* on Sunday nights were regular topics of conversation in neighborhoods and at work. Still ahead were the riveting national moments of the hearings on organized crime in 1951, which later made Estes Kefauver, an obscure Tennessee senator, into a potential vice-presidential candidate, and the Army-McCarthy hearings in 1954, in which establishment lawyers were the heroes of a tense daily drama that destroyed the influence of the maverick populist Senator Joe McCarthy of Wisconsin. These were the early equivalents of the O.J. Simpson trial and showed the power of television to crystallize national public opinion in a few days. Similar nationalized reactions were created in the aftermath of the Kennedy assassination in 1963 and in response to the riots at the Democratic convention in Chicago in 1968.

The definitive book about the impact of television on our politics has yet to be written, but it will surely emphasize the way in which confidence in government and political leaders has been undermined if not destroyed, the cost of campaigning for office driven through the roof (and our politics transformed thereby), and our foreign policy changed, perhaps for a very long time, by daily battlefield pictures from Vietnam. It is no coincidence that regular TV presentations of presidential debates and other political events began in 1960 and that voter turnout at elections has been declining ever since.

The presentation of "news," like any other TV programming, must be designed for the purpose of capturing and holding the passive viewer's attention in order to maximize advertising rates and income. To serve these purposes effectively, the news must stress such dimensions as shock, scandal, and entertainment, and it must not dwell too long on any one topic. From these criteria come the emphasis on government failures, corruption, or absurdity, and the now-dominating 30-second "soundbite," featuring the most outrageous allegations or name-calling that can be remotely justified at some later and less public moment.

But the most lasting effect of television on our politics stems from the absolute necessity for every candidate to purchase ever more expensive TV time for campaign advertising, often of a saturation level. With constituencies averaging more than 500,000 people, most candidates have little choice but to invest heavily in TV commercials. To attract and hold the viewer in the context of heavy competition, such commercials must be carefully (and expensively) crafted for maximum symbolic impact. For all these reasons, much of the officeholder's or candidate's time must be spent in fundraising, and he or she must depend totally on big-money contributors to win and hold office. No less important, the quality of political discourse suffers from the ruthless simplification required for television and the tendency to resort to character assassination.

Do continually expanding telecommunications have the potential to bring about an equivalent and reverse impact? In the development of telecommunications, we are about where television was in the 1950s, for many homes today remain without a computer or fax machine. However, awareness and usage of the new telecommunications modes are rapidly growing, and some form of interactive communication seems likely to be in almost every household within the next five years. Internet and e-mail experience are increasingly part of the business and educational worlds, and the personal computer is no longer merely for games and "computer nerds." The parallels with the evolution of television are clear: our fictional character Jeff (for Jefferson) is not far ahead of our times, and the revolution he helped to promote is already immanent in today's developments.

For the moment, we want to list the names and addresses of several groups—identified through the internet and by fax—that are currently working to promote versions of direct democracy and reformed representation. With help from interested readers, we plan to expand this list in the next edition. We anticipate that there will be many individuals and groups working out details of regular referendum proposals and new forms of representation at the state and local (or national) levels and several experiments on which to report. At the very least, there will be many more groups and organizations in the field and perhaps some significant movements under way. It is time for a clearinghouse function, and we will be glad to help as required. This is only a partial list, a start on a long road to the future.

Americans for Tax Reform Initiative Project. Washington, D.C. FAX: (202) 785-0261. Regular conference call-ins. WWW site: http://www.atr.org

Americans Talk Issues Foundation. Survey guidance. FAX: (904) 826-4196

Center for Living Democracy. RR 1, Black Fox Rd., Brattleboro, Vt. 05301. FAX: (802) 254-1227

Center for Voting and Democracy. Washington, D.C. Sponsors of several PR proposals and publishers of *Voting and Democracy Review.* FAX: (202) 727-8127

DemocracyDirect. "Cyberspace voting center" offers opportunities to vote on key issues. E-mail: neurotel@infoplaza.com

Democracy 2000. Newsletter: *Dialogue on Representation.* Sponsors of "Universal Representation" proposals. 71 Livingston Ave., Dobbs Ferry, N.Y. 10522. FAX: (914) 674-9113

Democratech Party (of British Columbia, Canada, and International). Calls for national popular decision making to replace elected politicians. E-mail: feedback@democratech.org

IRON Press, Inc. *Initiative and Referendum Organizers' Newsletter.* Carson City, Nev. FAX: (702) 885-9983

Teledemocracy Action News Network, Auburn University, Ala. FAX: (334) 844-6161

Voters' Bill of Rights. Seven legislative proposals for national initiative and referendum procedures. Office of Rep. Pete Hoekstra (R-Mich.), 1122 Longworth Office Building, Washington, D.C., 20515.

Bibliographic Essay

In this essay we have combined specific citations of sources for data and quotes contained in the text with an annotated bibliography of documents and materials that we found to be of particular help in developing this book. We have made no effort to include every work related to our topic, but only those from which we have gleaned some guidance or provocation. We assume that readers of this essay are citizens and students whose interests are in the problems, politics, and policies that we discuss, rather than specialists with concern for the nuances of difference between authors or the evolution of complex ideas across time. We do include references to books and other sources written from differing political perspectives, including several with whose arguments we disagree. And we draw quotes from a variety of sources, again including several with which we disagree or whose basic positions are at odds with the thrust of the quote cited.

Preface

Nationalism is a concept with many definitions and a long and sometimes lurid history that has produced a huge literature. Because of its association with xenophobic and authoritarian movements and regimes, we seriously considered avoiding it entirely. But the occasions of its explicit popularity in the United States have been interesting and important moments in our history, and we finally decided to define it carefully and then use it to distinguish ourselves from the dominant globalists.

The modern American usage of the concept stems from Edward Bellamy's utopian novel of 1889, *Looking Backward, 2000–1887* (Boston: Houghton Mifflin, 1889), in which Bellamy used the device of a man falling asleep in 1887 and awakening in the year 2000 to have major characters describe the new world. In that world, a benevolent national control over the distribution of wealth and income was exercised to assure the equality and happiness of all. Within two years of the book's publication, more than 150 "new nationalist" clubs were in existence to promote Bellamy's ideas.

The term was again employed during the Progressive era at the start of the twentieth century, apparently initially by Herbert Croly in *The Promise of American Life* (New York: Macmillan, 1909) as part of his effort to promote support for a Hamiltonian centralization of government. Croly wrote quite explicitly for Theodore Roosevelt, who made "The New Nationalism" the slogan for his 1912 presidential campaign. For TR, the term meant both domestic centralization and "carrying a big stick" in foreign policy.

Our usage fits neither of these, although we are attracted by the analogy to Bellamy's fictional presentation. We have stressed throughout, however, that ours is not what most of the others have been, that is, an authoritarian solution. We seek only to distinguish Americans and their interests from the global imagery that is essentially a cover for the interests of the transnational corporations and banks that dominate the world economy. (For further discussion of nationalism today, see the references associated with Michael Lind's work in chapter 1.)

Chapter 1. Thomas Jefferson Revisited:
The Fourth of July, 2000

The American middle class, particularly its values and economic circumstances, has been the object of much attention since the 1980s. No author has done more to portray the plight of the middle class than political columnist Kevin Phillips in *The Politics of Rich and Poor* (New York: Random House, 1990) and *Boiling Point: Democrats, Republicans, and the Decline of Middle-Class Prosperity* (New York: Random House, 1993). A more anecdotal study is that of the investigative reporters Donald L. Barlett and James B. Steele, *America: What Went Wrong?* (New York: Simon and Schuster, 1991). Much recent polling data are used to explore values, attitudes, and voting implications by Stanley B. Greenberg in *Middle Class Dreams: The Politics and Power of the New American Majority* (New York: Times Books, 1995). The middle class is at the center of Christopher Lasch's concern in *The Revolt of the Elites and the Betrayal of Democracy* (New York: Norton, 1995). An incisive essay making many of the points of this chapter is Michael Lind, "To Have and Have Not: Notes on the Progress of the American Class War," *Harper's Magazine,* June 1995, 35–47.

The data on wealth and income distribution are readily available in many sources, the most comprehensive being Phillips' *Boiling Point.* The most recent data are drawn from *Time's* Special Report, "The State of America, 1995," 30 January 1995, 60; and the *New York Times,* 17 April 1995, A1 and C4. The crime data are from the same edition of *Time,* 63.

The quote from Phillips may be found in *Boiling Point,* 111–12. The quote from Barlett and Steele is from *America: Who Really Pays the Taxes?* (New York: Simon and Schuster, 1994), 97. The articulation of renewal opportunities and confidence data is suggested by Greenberg, *Middle Class Dreams,* passim.

The best single source for understanding American ideology, particularly the points made about the dangers of factions and majorities, remains James Madison's famous essay No. 10 of *The Federalist,* originally written in 1787. Many editions of this celebrated work are readily available.

The consolidated quote from Jefferson is drawn from his Letter to Samuel Kercheval of July 1816 and will be found in any edition of his works. The last two sentences are from an earlier point in the same letter, and that is why we refer to the quote as "consolidated."

The other contemporary proposals for change that are briefly reviewed are now more fully described, in the same order. Alvin and Heidi Toffler, *Creating a New American Civilization: The Politics of the Third Wave* (Atlanta: Turner Publishing, 1995), is a brief (110 pages) and well-edited compilation drawn from three earlier books (*The Third Wave*, 1980; *Powershift*, 1990; and *War and Anti-War*, 1993), supplemented by two new chapters. The concept for the book, and the editing, came from Newt Gingrich's Progress & Freedom Foundation (see the Tofflers' "Authors' Note" on p. 111), and Gingrich contributed a five-page introduction extolling the book.

The basic thrust of the Tofflers' argument is similar to ours and concludes with a call for more direct democracy and decentralization, both taking advantage of new communication technology. Our reservations about their work stem from their lack of political sensitivity to the plight of the middle class and the polarization of wealth and income and to the dominating role of today's economic and political power structure, as well as their unwillingness to propose specific remedies that take these factors into account. For an interesting profile of the Tofflers that emphasizes their independence from Gingrich, see Claudia Dreifus, "Present Shock," in the *New York Times Magazine*, 11 June 1995, 46–50.

Michael Lind's *The Next American Nation: The New Nationalism and the Fourth American Revolution* (New York: Free Press, 1995) employs much the same basic analysis as we do, but does not address the question of what to do about it. His "nationalism" is a prediction without substantive detail or much sense of the process involved in accomplishing the requisite change. A better explanation of the meaning of "nationalism" may be found in a Lind essay coauthored with John B. Judis, "For a New Nationalism," *New Republic*, 27 March 1995, 19–27. Its "three pillars" are described as economic nationalism, national-interest realism in defense, and a nation-unifying approach to social policy—all of which amount to an appeal to "think and act anew," unencumbered by specifics.

Kevin Phillips's work of the past thirty years amounts to probably the most thorough and compelling analysis of the evolution and problems of American politics to be found anywhere. In *Arrogant Capital: Washington, Wall Street, and the Frustration of American Politics* (Boston: Little, Brown, 1994), he presents a valuable characterization of the grip on Washington, D.C., enjoyed by the newly global financial elite and offers some interesting suggestions for political changes that might restore greater popular control. How any of these might actually be implemented, however, will have to await publication of his next book.

In *United We Stand: How We Can Take Back Our Country* (New York: Hyperion, 1992), Ross Perot set forth a brief (118 pages) and ruthlessly simplified critique that amounted to his platform in the 1992 presidential campaign. In his view, the deficit was the touchstone, and all would be well if the voters elected him president. The charts are provocative, but middle-class entitlements are exclusively the problem, and political analysis is almost totally lacking.

No work does a more thoughtful job of examining federal-state relations than Alice Rivlin's *Reviving the American Dream: The Economy, the States, and the Federal Government* (Washington, D.C.: Brookings Institution, 1992). Rivlin, a former head of the Congressional Budget Office and currently the head of the president's Office of Management and Budget, makes the case for decentralizing federal functions and passing new federal revenues to the states. Her orientation is academic and technical, however, with little linkage to politics and no sense of social justice for the middle class.

Edward Luttwak, a conservative military strategist, turns his perspective loose on the economic decline of the United States in *The Endangered American Dream: How to Stop the United States from Becoming a Third World Country and How to Win the Geo-Economic Struggle for Industrial Supremacy* (New York: Simon and Schuster, 1993). Luttwak makes the argument that income polarization raises the prospect of Third World status, but he sees the problem as externally caused. He calls for a kind of moral restoration, with regressive federal taxes, enforced savings, and a more aggressive trade posture.

Newt Gingrich's *To Renew America* (New York: Harper's, 1995) is essentially a compilation of his now-familiar principles drawn from the "Contract with America," various speeches, and the college course he developed. Hedrick Smith's *Rethinking America: A New Game Plan from the American Innovators — Schools, Business, People, Work* (New York: Random House, 1995) is a prescription based on a reporter's interviews with "innovators." It is as detached from political analysis as Gingrich is sunk into day-to-day congressional practice.

Not one of the works cited here addresses the real-world fact that the American power structure does not *want* to give up its privileges, share its wealth and income, or drastically change the way things work. Every author, with the sole exception of Phillips, seems to assume that the powers that be are benign and ready to do what the author recommends as the right thing. There is no sense of conflict or difference of interest that sets the dominant elites apart from the rest of Americans. No author really takes up the cause of the American middle class as a matter of social justice or provides specific remedies for its plight. That is why we have written this book in the form that we offer it.

Chapter 2. The United States at the End of the Twentieth Century

The scope and character of the American transformation has been addressed repeatedly. The Tofflers' *Third Wave* (1980) is an example, as is Robert Reich's *The Work of Nations: Preparing Ourselves for 21st Century Capitalism* (New York: Knopf, 1991). An incisive and more recent version is Peter Drucker's *Post-Capitalist Society* (New York: HarperCollins, 1993). These and similar works all posit an ongoing global transformation to a knowledge society in which high technology dominates.

Kevin Phillips takes up the U.S. economic and cultural decline in chapter 3 of *Arrogant Capital*. Edward Luttwak's *The Endangered American Dream* is the most aggressive in detailing the extent of the relative economic decline of the United States, and it is his projections of eclipse and the date of American Third World status that we cite. Also, the most recent data alluding to simultaneous productivity increase and wage/benefit decline, raising the issue of the rising share claimed by capital over labor, can be found in the *New York Times*, 25 June 1995, E4.

The UN "Development Index" data are from "Taking Stock of Development," *Real World International,* November 1990, 44. The Phillips quote is from *Arrogant Capital,* 84. The union membership and real-wage data are from *U.S. News and World Report,* 26 December 1994–2 January 1995, 126. The Rudman-Tsongas quote is from p. 13 of their Foreword to Peter G. Peterson's *Facing Up: Paying Our Nation's Debt and Saving Our Children's Future* (New York: Simon and Schuster, 1993).

Chapter 3. Forward to the 1890s:
The Basic Scenarios

Images of the future also abound, about equally divided between wildly optimistic and grimly foreboding. An example of the former is the Special 1994 Bonus Issue of *Business Week* entitled "21st Century Capitalism." Our quote is drawn from this source, which does a quite respectable job of identifying different kinds of capitalism likely to develop in the near term. An example of the latter image of the future is Luttwak's *The Endangered American Dream,* chapter 4 of which bears the title, "When Will the United States Become a Third World Country?" Our quote is from p. 127 of this work.

Forecasting from existing trends may be dangerous because important shaping conditions can always change. On the other hand, current trends are all we have in the way of experience, and they can serve as at least a baseline—with the usual proviso, "all things remaining the same...." Thus we extend what appear to be stable trend lines, as probabilities but not predictions. All the data are from the Special Report, "The State of America,

1995" in *Time*, 30 January 1995, 63–68. The attorney general's quote is from p. 63. The data about children under eighteen and births by single mothers, as well as the summary quote from *Time*, are all from p. 54 of the same Special Report.

The materials on the Republican budget and policy implications are drawn from Stephen Moore, ed., *Restoring the Dream: The Bold New Plan by House Republicans* (New York: Times Books, 1995), passim. Another important source of Republican budget and policy intentions is John Kasich, *The People's Budget* (Washington, D.C.: The Progress and Freedom Foundation, 1995). For a more principled version of conservatism that explicitly calls for putting honesty and moral principle over electoral success, see David Frum, *Dead Right* (New York: Basic Books, 1994). The Treasury estimates were reported in the *New York Times*, 7 April 1995, A11.

Democratic aspirations are far less clear than those of the Republicans. Mostly, they trail the Republicans, nipping and complaining about details. One sharply contrasting counterproposal noted in the text is the Black and Progressive Caucus budget proposal that would balance the budget by 2002 in an entirely different manner from the Republicans. It may be found in the 18 May 1995 edition of the *Congressional Record*. The Ronald Steel quote is from the *Washington Post Weekly Edition*, 12–18 June 1995, 24.

Comparison with the late nineteenth century is being made with increasing frequency. The Judis-Lind article cited in chapter 1 makes it quite explicitly. The Michael Barone quote is from *U.S. News and World Report*, 14 November 1994, 44. The Walter Russell Mead quote is from "Forward to the Past," the *New York Times Magazine*, 4 June 1995, 49.

Chapter 4. An Economy for Americans — All Americans

The literature on the restoration of the American economy, while voluminous, suffers from a strange compartmentalization—even tunnel vision. For us, the central issue is the need for good jobs for Americans in the United States, followed by national policy that *expands* (rather than contracts, as has been the case for the past thirty years) the income share of the middle sectors of families. But no others seem to share this focus. The closest approaches are calls for increased savings, greater investment, and expanding productivity. The problems with such exhortations are that the middle class cannot save, even with two wage earners on the job; investment goes overseas, where the profits are higher; and productivity has taken a big jump, while wages and benefits declined sharply.

There is a large body of work around the theme of globalization, international trade, and the imperative of global competitiveness, which we believe serves chiefly to justify putting the interests of transnational corporations and banks ahead of those of American workers. And there is an even larger body of work that takes up the U.S. national debt and annual deficits as the core of the American economic problem. Almost all this work focuses on runaway "entitlements" and seeks to balance the budget by slashing Medicare, Medicaid, and Social Security.

Amid this relative wasteland, the Progressive Policy Institute's *Mandate for Change* offers a comprehensive menu that includes job promotion as one of several areas for new policy. See Will Marshall and Martin Schram, eds., *Mandate for Change* (New York: Berkley Books, 1993). Developed by the Clinton-sponsored institute as an agenda for the new administration, it stands in some respects as a signpost for routes not taken. A provocative "big picture" approach to areas not always seen together is Leon F. Bouvier and Lindsey Grant, *How Many Americans? Population, Immigration, and the Environment* (San Francisco: Sierra Club Books, 1994). The authors argue that the carrying capacity of the American environment requires reduction in immigration as a means of containing total population. Alice Rivlin's *Restoring the American Dream* offers a good standard bibliography on workforce training, education for competitiveness, and the like (pp. 183–87). The best of the entitlement-cutting prescriptions for balancing the federal budget is Peter G. Peterson, *Facing Up: Paying Our Nation's Debt and Saving Our Children's Future* (New York: Simon and Schuster, 1993).

Chapter 5. "Each Generation Has the Right to Choose for Itself"

The redesign of the structure of the American political system, a topic once immediately dismissed by all "realistic" thinkers as totally impracticable (and indeed, quite unnecessary) is now moving into the realm of serious discussion. Most often considered is the reallocation of functions from the federal government to the states. Alice Rivlin's *Reviving the American Dream* offers some sound decentralization proposals, plus an interesting idea for common-shared taxes among the states (chaps. 7 and 8). Kevin Phillips proposes both decentralization of functions and redistribution of federal offices around the country in *Arrogant Capital* (chap. 8).

Proportional voting has developed a substantial literature and is being actively promoted at several sites around the country. The best book on the subject is Douglas Amy, *Real Choices, New Voices* (New York: Columbia University Press, 1991). The Center for Voting and Democracy in Washington, D.C., monitors publications, court cases, and movement toward PR in various U.S. states and cities. See their newsletter, *Voting and Democracy Review,* published quarterly.

A national initiative and referendum procedure has been proposed by some advocates, most recently by Kevin Phillips in the work just cited. The Tofflers propose to go somewhat further in this direction through some unspecified constitutional change that would take advantage of electronic capabilities (see *Creating a New Civilization,* chap. 9). Campaign finance reform is often proposed, but the barrier erected by the Supreme Court when it held that campaign funding was a form of free speech has seemed insurmountable. In our view, all these important goals can and should be accomplished through constitutional amendments, and that is why we have offered discussion drafts for each purpose.

The extensive quote and the discussion following it are from Greenberg's *Middle Class Dreams,* 250–54. Later quotes are from Peterson, *Facing Up,* 191, 197.

Chapter 6. The New American Democracy

As far as we know, we stand alone as advocates of a systematic means for regular national voting on major issues. The implications of instituting such a procedure (after testing in several states, of course) are vast, as the text suggests. We think our proposal is consistent with the aspirations voiced by the Tofflers and responds directly to the needs for restoring middle-class significance articulated by Christopher Lasch in *The Revolt of the Elites* (New York: Norton, 1995), 45. We think it is responsive also to the need for increased middle-class electoral power expressed by Robert Wiebe in his recent *Self-Rule: A Cultural History of American Democracy* (Chicago: University of Chicago Press, 1995). We argue that it is fully consistent with Jefferson's oft-stated trust in the people, an example of which is quoted from a 1787 letter to Madison. In the same letter, Jefferson flatly declares: "It is my principle that the will of the majority should always prevail."

But we expect this proposal to be the most controversial of all those made in our book, and we look forward to years of dialogue on the subject.

As a final bibliographic item and one with important substantive impact, we want to note a major work appearing after our manuscript was delivered to the publisher. The authors are Sol Erdman and Lawrence Susskind, whose book is titled *Reinventing Congress for the 21st Century* (New York: Frontier Press, 1995). The scope of their proposals, which flow from the work of the MIT-Harvard Public Disputes Program, is considerably larger than the title suggests. Essentially, they seek to reconstruct the concepts of representation itself, converting it from single-member geographically grounded districts to at-large elections in which winners reflect the range of popular beliefs and preferences. The means of doing so is a form of proportional representation called "universal representation," in which all candidates run at large on the basis of personal platforms reflecting their personal values and beliefs. Voters have first, second, and third preferences recorded for allocation and reallocation of their votes as the candidates with the lowest vote totals are progressively eliminated until all open seats are filled. Each representative is directly accountable to a group of citizens who share common concerns. The legislative body's system of organization (usually committees) is based on the commitment to represent all viewpoints, appropriately weighted according to the number of supporting constituents, in a negotiating process that is intended to produce a result maximally acceptable to all parties.

These proposals are particularly significant for at least three reasons. First, they provide a form of proportional representation readily adaptable to American political culture and its anti-party, anti-ideological premises, and one that has far better chances of adoption than the available others. Second, they offer a means for formulating the ballot questions that would go to the voters in our regular referendums that is popularly grounded and therefore superior to the nonpartisan routes that we proposed in the text. Third, the inevitably important tasks of implementing popular decisions would be in the hands of more genuinely representative elected officials.

The combination of regular referendums with universal representation strikes us as the basis for a new "deliberative democracy" that synthesizes the best and most current forms of direct democracy and representative democracy. We look forward to testing periods for such new forms in local and state settings and, once refined through such experience, at the national level.

Illustrations

The authors and publisher acknowledge with thanks the institutions, firms, and individuals that supplied the illustrations for this book.

Index